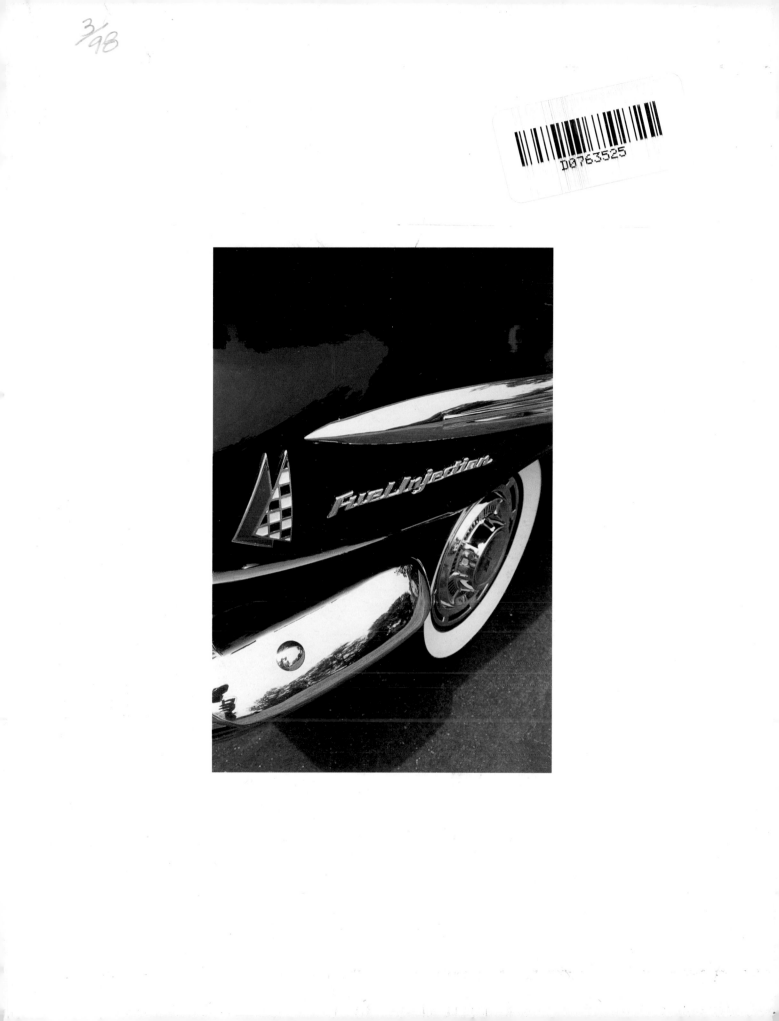

FIFTIES MUSCLE

The Dawn of High Performance

Mike Mueller

Motorbooks International
Publishers & Wholesalers ®

ACKNOWLEDGMENTS

THAT this not-so-humble scribe was given the task of putting together a book on American performance cars of the '50s represented a reach of sorts, considering I was not even one year old when that decade ended. What could this kid (thank you so much) possibly know about these cars?, you might ask. First off, I know that most guys my age have very little perspective when going back in time to drive those high-horsepower chariots of the Fabulous Fifties, especially after having grown accustomed to today's latest techno-crazy machines. Having done time behind the wheel of various vintage vehicles from solid-axle Corvettes to two-seat T-birds, from fuel-injected Bel Airs, to Tri Power Pontiacs; I must say that progress is a wonderful thing. How did drivers handle all that horsepower some four decades ago with that slow steering, those humble brakes, the meek rubber, and the compromised chassis?

Then again, perhaps car owners today are far too removed from the driving process, a situation that commonly leads many careless drivers to a false sense of confidence. You knew where you stood behind the wheel of a hot car in 1955—if you couldn't handle the heat, you had no business in the kitchen. Today's cars are so forgiving and driver friendly, even my grandma could run circles around some of the '50s best performing cars without even knowing whose toes she was stepping on. Improved tire technology alone has made racers out of all of us these days. And many inexperienced drivers pay the price when they finally find out just how far today's massive treads will allow them to run unaware beyond their own personal limits.

Chrysler dominated the '50s horsepower race, thanks to its legendary "hemi" V-8, introduced in 1951. Four years later, the first of Chrysler's fabled letter-series cars, the C-300, debuted to showcase hemi power in proud fashion.

Although the '50s ledger was also full of foolish accident reports inspired by high horsepower, the fine line then existing between confident control and tragic consequences probably kept more of the little dogs on the porch. Running with the big boys back then required more skill, more confidence, and more understanding of just what those bias-ply tires could (or couldn't) do when fully stressed. And make no mistake about it, some of those wallowing, bucking broncos could stress some rubber in a serious way.

Much of what I learned at an early age concerning that last fact came from my father, Jim Mueller, Sr. Unlike me, he grew up knowing all about just how hot '50s cars were. For as long as I can remember, I've heard him speak fondly of the '55 Chevy his brother once owned. Nothing was hotter, at least as far as he was concerned. Some did come close, however, like his brother in law's J 2 Oldsmobile or his other brother's Golden Hawk Stude. Later, dad became a Pontiac man just about the time the big Wide Tracks were taking over American roads. He has basically owned Ponchos ever since. And just last year he nearly floored me when he came home with a fully loaded (blaring CD player and all) Grand Prix sport coupe. How does the Hot One stack up now, Dad?

Basically everything I know about cars, old or new, I owe to Jim Mueller, thanks to his persistent demands that I get out there (usually in the snow) and get those broken-down heaps I was always driving in my teens back on the road. Somehow, it was that grease-beneath-the-fingernails experience that eventually led to a career in automotive journalism. Who'd a-thunk it? Certainly not Dad, not after all the grief I gave him for 20 years or so. Nice trade, huh Dad? I'd say I couldn't have done it without you, but you know I'd never admit to that.

I will, on the other hand, readily admit such a thing to the many other people who helped make this

7

The author's father, Jim Mueller, Sr., fulfilling his need for speed on his brother Ed's Whizzer bicycle, circa 1951. Once on four wheels later in the decade, he would lose his heart to Studebaker's Golden Hawks and Bunkie Knudsen's Wide Tracks from Pontiac.

wandering epic possible. Great guys (translated: free labor) like my brother Dave Mueller in Flatville, Illinois; brother-in-law Frank Young in Savoy, Illinois; and Frank's boy Jason helped make various photo shoots in the Midwest last year all that easier. And more enjoyable. Also, I'd better take this time to mention Mom, Nancy Mueller, for keeping the light on at the old family homestead outside Champaign, Illinois, during my various stays there during those photo junkets. That's right, Ma, I was diligently working all those nights until three in the morning.

Additional thanks go to all my friends who helped locate the great automobiles you'll see on these pages. Ever-present Ray Quinlan in Champaign typically dropped everything to help, as did fellow hometowners Max Dilley and Elmer Lash. Here in the Lakeland, Florida, area, Bill Tower did the same, as he has every time I've called. I can't thank you enough, Bill.

Jim Benjaminson of the Plymouth Owners Club in Walhalla, North Dakota, was also more than ready, willing, and able to help, as were Karla Rosenbusch and former cohort John Heilig at *Automobile Quarterly* in Kutztown, Pennsylvania. Others who helped point me in the right direction towards the specific cars I needed to photograph include Richard Quinn of the Studebaker Drivers Club in Mokena, Illinois; T-bird man Dick Cavanaugh of Longwood, Florida; Betty Dworschack of the Nash Car Club of America in Clinton, Iowa; and Nash club member Robert Cosgrove of Port St. Lucie, Florida.

Corvette sources came from Brent Ferguson of the Classic Corvettes of Orlando Club here in Florida and Robin Winnan at Harmony Corvette in Marengo, Illinois. Speaking of Corvettes, I owe many thanks to Ellen Kliene at the Indianapolis Motor Speedway Hall of Fame Museum, Indianapolis, Indiana, and Dan Gale of the National Corvette Museum (NCM) in Bowling Green, Kentucky, for allowing me a once-in-a-lifetime chance to spend some up-close-and-personal time with Zora Duntov's fabled 1957 SS racer. NCM men Danny Gillock, Tim Reilly, and Patrick Hayes were also of great assistance during that shoot outside the Bowling Green Museum two falls ago.

Another tip of the hat goes to musclecar collector Milton Robson and his righthand man, Wayne Allen, in Gainesville, Georgia.

Historical photographic support came from many sources, including Pontiac guru Paul Zazarine of Dobbs Publishing Group (DPG) here in Lakeland. DPG's Donald Farr, Tom Shaw (editor, *Musclecar Review*), and Greg Pernula (editor, *Corvette Fever*) were also unfailingly cooperative when I came a demanding. Curator Mark Patrick of The National Automotive History Collection at the Detroit Public Library amazed me with his wonderful willingness to fulfill my requests, with great haste no less. The same can be said for Corvette restoration expert Noland Adams in California; Jonathan Mauk of the Daytona Racing Archives in Daytona Beach, Florida; Brandt Rosenbusch at Chrysler Historical in Detroit; and veteran automotive writer Robert Ackerson in Schenevus, New York. Finally, I surely owe more than one lunch to Publications International's Will Fox in Chicago, who, along with his comrades at PI's *Collectible Automobile* magazine, publisher Frank Peiler and r&d man Mitch Frumkin, has responded to my pleas on short notice more than once now.

Equally supportive were my ever-ready photo technician friends, Rob Reaser (another Dobbs man) and Ollie Young, both of Lakeland. Rob and Ollie's hard work helped make my job quite a bit easier—and my wallet quite a bit lighter. Don't spend it all in one place, guys. A hearty handshake also goes to local Hooters manager and cheesehead-wearin' Packer-backer Tom Radakovitz, who somehow managed to help keep what was left of my social life alive during the last half of 1995 while this book (and others) was going together, late as usual.

Finally, I must offer my appreciation to all the car owners who not only gave me their valuable time but also helped make those various 5000-mile trips much more fun than work should be. Thanks to these men and women, I may never have to get a real job again. In general order of appearance, this list includes:

1955 Chrysler C300, Otto and Mary Rosenbusch, Rochester Hills, Michigan; 1955 Chevrolet Bel Air, Bill and Barbara Jacobsen, Silver Dollar Classic Cars, Odessa, Florida; 1919 Ford Model T racer, Dennis Gunning, Tuscola, Illinois; 1932 Chrysler speedster, Sam Mann, Fairlawn, New Jersey; 1950 Oldsmobile 88 Holiday coupe, Gene and Marilyn Roy, Casselberry, Florida; 1954 Nash Ambassador, Brian Bauske, Gainesville, Florida; 1954 Hudson Hornet convertible, Frank and Carol Childs, Boca Raton, Florida; 1952 Lincoln Capri convertible, Carl and Mary Allen, Naples, Florida; 1956 Dodge D500 convertible, Bruce and Karen Faulkner, Lakeland, Florida; 1956 Corvette SR-2, Bill and Betty Tower, Plant City, Florida; 1957 Corvette SS, Indianapolis Motor Speedway Hall of Fame Museum, Indianapolis, Indiana; 1957 Ford Fairlane supercharged sedan and 1957 Chevrolet *Black Widow* racer, Floyd Garrett, Fernandina Beach, Florida; 1950 Skorpion, Era Harvey, Leesburg, Florida; 1953 Muntz Jet, Fred and Lynn Hunter, Ft. Lauderdale, Florida; 1953 Nash-Healey, Paul Sable, Fleetwood, Pennsylvania; 1954 Kaiser-Darrin, Edwin Hobart, Naples, Florida; 1954 Chevrolet Corvette, Bill Warner, Jacksonville, Florida; 1955 Chevrolet Corvette, Elmer and Dean Puckett, Elgin, Illinois; 1955 Ford Thunderbird, Jim and Carol Lytle, Gotha, Florida; 1956 Ford Thunderbird, Richard Woodworth, Tolono, Illinois; 1957 Ford Thunderbird "F-code," Kevin and Shellie O'Hara, Orlando, Florida; 1957 Chevrolet Corvette "Airbox," Milton Robson, Gainesville, Florida; 1958 Corvette, Ron Cenowa, Shelby Township, Michigan; 1955 Studebaker President Speedster, Harold Goepferich, Dallas Center, Iowa; 1955 Packard Caribbean convertible, Kathy Pinkerton, Hillsborough Beach, Florida; 1955 Plymouth Belvedere, Art Ubbens, Lake Wales, Florida; 1956 Chevrolet Bel Air 225 horsepower V-8, Fred Gaugh, Polk City, Florida, and Terry Sheafer and Jerome Cain, Lakeland, Florida; 1956 Studebaker Golden Hawk, Frank and Anita Ambrogio, Casselberry, Florida; 1956 Dodge D500 hardtop, Bruce and Karen Faulkner, Lakeland, Florida; 1956 Plymouth Fury, Tom and Glenda Pike, Springfield, Missouri; 1956 DeSoto Pacesetter convertible, E. R. and Estella Dorsett, Terre Haute, Indiana; 1957 Studebaker Golden Hawk, Don McCullen, Gainesville, Florida; 1957 Pontiac Star Chief Tri Power, Pete Mazzochi, Naples, Florida; 1957 Oldsmobile 88 convertible J-2, 1957 Pontiac Bonneville convertible, and 1957 Chevrolet Nomad fuel injected, Bill and Barbara Jacobsen, Silver Dollar Classic Cars, Odessa, Florida; 1959 Chevrolet Impala convertible 348/four-speed and 1959 Chevrolet Impala convertible fuel injected, Dick Hubbard, Monticello, Indiana; 1959 Plymouth Sport Fury, Ken Lanious, Forest Park, Illinois.

Thank you, all.

INTRODUCTION

AMERICANS' NEED FOR SPEED
Performance Prehistory

IN the minds of most car buffs these days, the so-called "musclecar" era officially began in 1964 with Pontiac's introduction of its feared and revered GTO, a car built only to go fast. The idea itself was simple. Take your hottest big V-8 and stuff it into your not-so-big mid-sized model. Throw in a few bits of heavy-duty hardware, maybe an image piece or two, and keep the bottom line down where young Americans hungry for horsepower can reach it. As for potential customers with fatter wallets and a bigger itch, try offering a high-powered scratch in the form of a long list of potent options. Presto, instant muscle-bound machine, just the car Detroit's automakers in the early '60s were waiting for to ride the crest of this country's postwar baby-boomer wave, which had just then reached legal driving age.

Once the GTO was loose on the streets in 1964, many rivals quickly appeared. Buick's Gran Sport. Oldsmobile's 4-4-2. Chevrolet's Chevelle Super Sport. Even smaller, lighter ponycars also flexed their muscles: Ford's Mustang GT and Plymouth's Barracuda, followed later by Chevy's Camaro Z28 and Pontiac's Firebird 400. Et cetera, et cetera.

More outrageous machines began appearing as Detroit's horsepower race really got running in the late '60s. "Hemi" Mopars. Ford Cobra Jets and Boss Mustangs. Pontiac's Trans Am. Chevy's SS 396 and 427 Vettes. By 1970, the industry's top engine displacement had reached 455 cubic inches (Buick, Olds,

They didn't call this machine the "Hot One" for nothing. Although there were cars faster and more powerful on Mainstreet U.S.A. in 1955, the all-new Chevy emerged as one of the first American automobiles to offer real performance to the average buyer.

and Pontiac), and Chevrolet's fearsome LS-6 SS 454 Chevelle was offering John Q. Public 450 real horses. The equally real possibility of a street car (with more than two seats) breaking into the 12-second bracket for the quarter mile loomed large that year.

But even as these brutes were first leaving the line, it had become apparent that the great American horsepower race had run its course within socially acceptable parameters. After 1970, federal lawmakers finally saw fit to pull in the reins on runaway performance, something many safety-conscious legislators in Washington had been calling for with great vigor since almost a decade before the GTO was born. Even if safety crusaders hadn't finally won the day, the musclecar breed would've never survived the ever-tightening limitations imposed by tougher emissions standards resulting from the various clean air acts of the '60s and '70s. Skyrocketing insurance rates also helped spell doom for American performance. Horsepower hounds first noticed a downturn in 1971 when compression ratios were dropped across the board in Detroit. Three years later it was all over but the shouting.

With so much having happened so quickly in the American performance arena during the '60s, it became too easy to overlook the plain fact that Detroit's horsepower race did not begin in 1964. From a "modern musclecar" perspective, perhaps a leg of it did. But the whole shooting match can be traced back almost all the way to the end of World War II.

Performance Sells
With a rapidly changing postwar market at hand, this country's auto-making elite were at first able to sell anything on wheels in '46 and '47 as demand simply

Henry Ford's interest in racing dominated his early automaking efforts. Here, he poses with legendary driver Barney Oldfield at the tiller of the "999" racer in October 1902. Oldfield had just driven the 999 to victory at the Manufacturers' Cup Race at Grosse Pointe, Michigan.

overwhelmed supply. But the forces of competition quickly caught up, an economic reality most in the industry had been preparing for even before peace broke out. It was obvious that all-new approaches to selling cars would be needed if a company wanted to remain a player in the modern postwar market once the initial peacetime feeding frenzy subsided. And fresh styling wouldn't be enough; customers expected that.

So it was that the American auto-making crowd fell back on a long-standing, reliable sales ploy, an attraction as old as the automobile itself—performance. Performance, as in speed. The more speed, the more sales. And to get more speed, automakers obviously needed more power. It was this need for speed that helped kick off Detroit's horsepower race, which was just getting underway as the '40s were winding down.

Before the war, American buyers rarely were presented with a car boasting anything more than 100 horses. But by 1951, the industry's average output rating had reached 132.7 horsepower. That average continued rising, hitting 148.1 in 1953, then soared to 208.2 horses two years later. With its hemispherical combustion chambers (thus the nickname "hemi"), Chrysler's innovative Firepower V-8 had become the industry's output leader in 1951 at an impressive 180 horsepower, this coming from 331 cubic inches.

Former leader Cadillac took back that rightful honor in 1952, raising the output ante to 190 horses, and followed suit again the following year with its 210-horsepower 331-cubic-inch V-8. Chrysler jumped back on top in 1954, boosting its hemi horses to 235 before things really started getting crazy in 1955. Chrysler would remain Detroit's power leader until 1958.

Top speed, coincidentally, was also on the rise, although at an understandably lesser rate, as not all that added horsepower was meant to come into play at the upper reaches of the performance curve. In 1951, the average top speed for American cars was 89.7 miles per hour. The following year, it was 96.1, and in 1954 it surpassed the magical 100-mile-per-hour barrier for the first time. By 1955, the industry average had reached 103.7 miles per hour, and the horsepower race was off and running at full tilt.

Later that year, *Motor Trend*'s John Booth took a shot at explaining what made that race tick in the '50s. "Every automobile manufacturer is in the business of making money," he wrote in the November 1955 issue. "It just so happens that he manufactures cars to make his money and, in order to sell his product, it must meet the approval of a majority of potential purchasers. Most automobile buyers today want as much power as the manufacturer can supply. If one make

One of America's earliest sports cars was the low-slung, powerful "T-head" Mercer Raceabout, shown here in stripped, ready-to-race form at Indianapolis in 1911. At the wheel is veteran Mercer team driver Hughie Hughes. Mercer built Raceabouts through 1914. *Courtesy Indianapolis Motor Speedway Archives*

offers more engine output at a competitive price than another, John Doe will buy the more powerful unit. This has created a competitive race among the manufacturers which, though accelerated the last few years, has been going on since the creation of man."

"Accelerated" was an understatement. Chrysler that year released Detroit's first "modern" (that is, post-war) 300-horsepower engine and then commemorated the event by naming the car it went into after that achievement. Chrysler's famed "letter-series" 300 models were the most powerful machines running on Mainstreet U.S.A. in the '50s and were still a formidable force in the '60s before becoming extinct after 1965.

Chrysler's second-edition letter car, the 1956 300B, established another first for the Motor City. Its optional 354-cubic-inch Firepower V-8 was rated at 355 horsepower. It was America's first engine to reach, at least on paper, the one-horsepower-per-cubic-inch plateau, an output level thought all but impossible just a few years previously. Chevrolet then became the second U.S. automaker to make that grade, introducing its fabled 283-horsepower 283-cubic-inch "fuelie" V-8 for both the Corvette and the passenger-car line in 1957. The Bow-Tie boys wasted little time laying claim to being the first to explore the

Probably most recognized from the World War I era was the Stutz Bearcat, a sporty machine appearing quite similar to the Mercer. Like the Raceabout, the Stutz Bearcat also used a T-head engine. This is a 1916 Bearcat. *Courtesy National Automotive History Collection, Detroit Public Library*

one-horsepower-per-cubic-inch stratosphere, and Chevy fans over the years have continually referred—however mistakenly—to their favorite marque as the high-powered pioneer in this area. The truth has since been buried beneath the years.

Clearly, automakers of the '50s were no strangers to performance, although with all things being relative,

Automakers learned early on that victories in competition could quickly lead to sales success on the street. Many companies, large and small, invested considerable cash in racing efforts in the years before World War I. These investments didn't always produce wins at the track and occasionally helped only to bring the parent firm to its knees. Such was the case for the Rayfield Company, of Chrisman, Illinois. Rayfield's aerodynamic racer, shown here at Indianapolis in May 1914, appeared promising, but broke down before it could prove itself. The company itself followed suit soon afterward. At the wheel—William Rayfield is in the co-pilot seat—is the ever-present Hughie Hughes, who Rayfield had hired away from Mercer that year.

the type of performance then being offered wouldn't necessarily wow someone who grew up with the GTO. While engines were indeed powerful, especially during the latter half of the decade, brakes on '50s cars were not. Nor were most chassis designs well suited to handle all that power in anything other than a straight line. Tire technology was also slow in catching up, with the rubber used generally not able to stand the higher and higher speeds made possible by higher and higher horsepower.

Progress, however, must start somewhere, and the engineering and design refinements of the '50s certainly represented welcomed improvements over what car buyers had experienced previously. Additionally, trying to compare apples with oranges picked a decade or two apart will always leave a bad taste in the mouths of those old enough to have seen the tree when it was just a sapling. Translated, the parents of today's baby boomers were every bit as excited about the top performing cars of the '50s in their day as their offspring would be concerning the more modern musclecars a decade or two later.

And believe it or not, some of those cars of the '50s could downright get it. Easily the best of the

breed was Chevrolet's Corvette, a sporting machine head and shoulders above its contemporaries as far as handling and sheer acceleration was concerned. By 1957, the hottest injected Corvettes were dipping well into the 6-second range for the 0–60 run at a time when 10 seconds represented the main measuring stick for a truly hot American performance machine.

Discounting a few limited-production sportsters, no stock, mainstream automobile out of Detroit had run faster than 10 seconds from rest to 60 miles per hour before 1955. The first V-8-powered Corvette broke that barrier in 1955, as did Chrysler's big C-300 and Chevy's passenger-line models with their optional 180-horsepower V-8. The following year, they were joined by Ford's Thunderbird, Studebaker's Golden Hawk, Plymouth's Fury, Dodge's D-500, and Buick's Century. Then, in 1957, 13 of the 24 cars *Motor Trend* tested did 0–60 in less than 10 seconds. Second behind the Corvette's sensational 6.4-second clocking was, amazingly enough, the Rambler Rebel four-door hardtop—a "street sleeper" if there ever was one—at 7.5 seconds.

Behind the deceptively quick Rebel came a long list of automobiles capable of claiming the title of performance car. Early stars of the '50s fast lane included Oldsmobile's Rocket 88—a much lighter cradle than a Cadillac for General Motors's newly designed overhead-valve V-8—and Hudson's Hornet with its antiquated, yet potent L-head six-cylinder powerplant. When Lincoln introduced its first modern overhead-valve V-8 in 1952, its luxury showboats instantly became high-speed haulers. And how can anyone forget what happened to grandpa's Chevrolet when chief engineer Ed Cole dropped an overhead-valve V-8 beneath the hood in 1955? They didn't call the reborn '55 Chevy the "Hot One" for nothing.

Even hotter were various special-edition models that came after Chevrolet's startling transformation. Following in the Chrysler 300's tire tracks were Plymouth's Fury, Dodge's D-500, and DeSoto's Adventurer, a high-energy, high-profile trio that debuted in 1956. In 1957, Pontiac introduced "Tri Power" and rolled out its fuel-injected Catalina, Oldsmobile first offered its triple-carb J-2 option, and Studebaker added a Paxton supercharger to its Golden Hawk, as did Ford for its two-seat Thunderbird.

By the time the tire smoke had cleared at decade's end, the industry's top engine displacement had surpassed 400 cubic inches and maximum advertised output had reached that same figure. Of course, much of this growth was simply due to the fact that Detroit needed bigger, stronger engines to power its bigger, accessory-laden automobiles. That some of these showboats just happened to be relatively fast as well as luxurious simply represented icing on the cake.

So what if the '60s were faster? The "Fabulous Fifties" were, at the time, fast enough. But this

Top performance in the automobile's early years was largely the province of the wealthy, leaving the masses to fend for themselves. No problem. Many creative wrench-turners simply made the best of what they had. Lightweight, cheap, and plentiful, Ford's Model T was a popular choice for this country's early hot rodders. This stripped-down 1919 T features many pre-Depression hot rod tricks, as well as various aftermarket performance pieces.

RIGHT
Ford's four-cylinder flathead engine was the weapon of choice for many early racers in the days before Dearborn introduced its V-8 flathead in 1932. Modifications shown here include both vintage '20s aftermarket parts and fabrications common to that era.

decade by no means represented the beginning for American performance.

Speed "Since the Creation of Man"

Man's need for speed was certainly nothing new when the modern postwar horsepower race began. As *Motor Trend*'s John Booth had said, this phenomenon had existed "since the creation of man." Without a doubt, even as Og the Neanderthal was chiseling out his first wheel, his buddy Gog down the street was undoubtedly hard at work hammering out a faster one. Then, once horse power evolved, one stallion would never do for the discriminating chariot driver, especially if you were a proud Roman running up against Charlton Heston in the arena at Circus Maximus.

About 18 centuries later came some of the earliest recorded speed standards, not on land but in water, driven by the wind. Record trans-oceanic crossings especially began piling up in the 1850s once steam started replacing sails. But the really big news as far as powered motivation was concerned came in the 1890s with the arrival of the horseless carriage and its new-fangled internal-combustion engine.

Early Automotive Speed Contests

Gas-powered contraptions had barely made their presence known in the horse-dominated world when the first competitive events began springing up. In November 1895, Hieronymous Mueller, of Decatur, Illinois, took his modified German-built Benz gasoline carriage north for a 50-mile run from Chicago to Evanston and back sponsored by the *Chicago Times-Herald*. This event was America's first officially sanctioned automobile race. The Mueller-Benz ended up finishing second, thanks to the efforts of a nearly frozen Charles Brady King, who by the way was the first man to build and drive a four-wheeled internal-combustion machine on the streets of Detroit. After completing his historic tour on March 6, 1896, King was rewarded with threats of a citation from local police for disturbing the peace.

Following King's vehicle that day, on a bicycle, was another young Detroit mover and shaker, Henry Ford. Three months later, Ford first operated his gas-powered "quadricycle" on June 4, 1896. Two years after that, on July 24, 1898, he founded the Detroit Automobile Company, which soon foundered and closed its doors in January 1901.

Left on his own, Ford then began working on his true passion, race cars. As expected, racing had already demonstrated itself as being the best route towards gaining public confidence, something the automobile hadn't yet secured. At the turn of the century, the hottest ticket in American automobiles came from the Winton company, this country's third largest auto manufacturer behind Locomobile and Columbia. Ford's goal was to beat Alexander Winton at this own game, which he did in a head-to-head race at Grosse Pointe, Michigan, on October 10, 1901. Henry's average speed for the 10-mile event was 43.5 miles per hour. He had promised his racer could do a mile a minute, the automotive world's first major performance barrier, which was soon afterward shattered

Henry Ford began offering affordable V-8 power to the budget-conscious customer in 1932. Manufactured in various sizes, the tried-and-true "flathead" V-8 survived up through 1953 before Dearborn finally opted for a modern, overhead-valve V-8.

(from a Yankee perspective) by America's first great race driver, Barney Oldfield.

Oldfield was the pilot for Ford's second, and most famous race car, the fabled 999, named after a record-setting New York Central railroad locomotive. One of two similar bare-frame racers, Ford's 999 featured an enormous four-cylinder engine displacing 1,156 cubic inches. Early problems with that engine led Ford to sell out his interests in the 999 project to his partner, Tom Cooper, who then ironed out the bugs and returned to Grosse Pointe in November 1902. There, with Oldfield aboard, the 999 beat a Winton for the second time, giving Henry Ford additional publicity even though he was basically no longer involved with the car. From there, young Henry had nowhere to go but up.

As Benson Ford later explained in 1962, "At the turn of the century, my grandfather built the Old 999, the world's first great racing car, and raced it with the immortal Barney Oldfield at the tiller—performing miracles unheard of in its time. The publicity from his racing efforts attracted the capital that enabled him to create Ford Motor Company. It is interesting to speculate how history might have turned, had it not been for the Old 999 and the fearless Barney Oldfield."

Still don't believe racing improves the breed?

Not to be outdone by Henry Ford, Alexander Winton continued his high-speed pursuits, traveling in April 1902 from his Cleveland plant to Daytona Beach, Florida's, northern neighbor, Ormond Beach, soon to be known as the "Birthplace of Speed." On the

Sporty performance in the '30s remained a luxury for the upper class as high-profile, high-priced Duesenbergs, Auburns, and Cords dominated the speed scene. The sky was the limit as long as you had the cash. Or friends in high places. This unique custom-bodied '32 Chrysler was factory built for Walter P. Chrysler's son, Walter P., Jr. Along with ultrasleek bodywork, this speedster also features a special high-compression straight-eight powerplant pumping out 160 horses, 35 more than stock.

hard sands there, Winton met up with Ransom E. Olds and proceeded to kick off a competition legacy for the area that still runs strong today. Both the Winton and Oldsmobile were clocked at 57 miles per hour that day—not a record, but it was a start.

In 1903, another Winton kicked up the Ormond sands to the tune of 68.98 miles per hour, a new standard for an American driving an American car. The first American to set a world record in an American machine came in 1906 at Ormond Beach when Fred Marriott piloted a Stanley Steamer to 127 miles per hour over the hard-packed sands. After Europeans recaptured the world speed record, Ralph DePalma brought it back to the U.S. in 1919 with a 149.875-mile-per-hour run down Ormond Beach in a twin-six Packard. The next year, Tommy Milton did DePalma

one better at Ormond, running 156.046 in a 16-cylinder Duesenberg Special. Ormond Beach's last record attempt came in 1935, after which time the land speed record scene moved from Florida to the salt beds of Bonneville in Utah, where it remains today.

But Ormond Beach wasn't the only proving grounds where this country's early automakers tried to impress prospective buyers with just how fast their cars could run. Among the most impressive cars of the day came from companies such as Lozier, Simplex, Moon, Marion, and Chadwick. In the years before World War I, these and many others were entered in all kinds of competitions; hillclimbs, endurance runs, around board tracks, and so on. Brighton Beach, Elgin, Long Island's Vanderbilt Cup, and Mt. Washington's "Climb to the Clouds" were just a few of the more famous places and events involved with early American performance demonstrations.

Easily the most famous came to be in August 1909 in an Indiana prairie four miles outside downtown Indianapolis. Two years later, the 2.5-mile Indianapolis Speedway first featured the event that would bring it real fame. Driving his Marmon Wasp, Ray Harroun won Indianapolis' first 500-mile Memorial Day International Sweepstakes, then billed as "the greatest automobile race ever run in the history of the industry." Who cared that "history" at the time only spanned a decade or so? The Indy 500 did indeed quickly become the "greatest spectacle in motorsports."

Early Indy 500s featured more than one relatively stock American entry. In 1912, the second running of the Memorial Day Sweepstakes was won by a local boy driving a local car, Joe Dawson in his Indianapolis-built National, probably the closest thing to a stock passenger car ever to turn a lap around "The Brickyard."

The year before, the first Indianapolis 500-miler had been a showcase for the car most consider America's first great performance machine, the Mercer Raceabout. Two stripped-down Mercers were entered in 1911, and both completed the race without ever having to unbelt their hoods. After the race that May, both Raceabouts were refitted with their lights, fenders, and running boards, and driven home.

Mercer's low, long Raceabout was powered by engineer Finley Robertson Porter's "T-head" four-cylinder engine, a valve-in-block design that featured an intake valve on one side of each cylinder, the corresponding exhaust valve on the other to create a "T" formation. The Porter-designed T-head displaced 300 cubic inches and produced a then-healthy 58 horsepower at 1700 rpm. Reported top speed was a sensational 70 miles per hour. But the Raceabout not only could fun fast, it also handled as well as anything then on American roads, thanks to its relative light weight and low-slung chassis. By most accounts, the original Mercer Raceabout, built from 1911 (introduced in late 1910) to 1914, was America's first great sports car.

America's second great sports car came in 1912 from the company former Marion Motor Car chief engineer Harry Stutz had founded in Indianapolis the previous year. Stutz's famed Bearcat was quite similar in appearance to the Mercer Raceabout. Like the Mercer, the Bearcat was low and lithe, with wide-open seating only for two and a T-head engine up front. But the Stutz had more engine under its folding hood and was slightly faster.

In 1917, the Stutz Bearcat was restyled and was fitted with an even more powerful 80-horsepower 360-cubic-inch four-cylinder engine. Most notable about this engine was its new T-head design that featured four valves per cylinder—no, multi-valve engines are not a new phenomenon. Neither are over-

head valves, overhead cams, tuned exhausts, dual ignition systems, and close-ratio four-speed transmissions—all these approaches were tried more than once in various designs before 1920.

Yet even with various valid innovations, basic engine layout remained relatively crude and inefficient for most cars during the first few decades of the twentieth century. Its four-valves-per-cylinder status aside, the Stutz engine was still a T-head, which meant the valves were situated in a less-than-desirable location within the cylinder block. The T-head design did allow the use of much larger valves (in some case as big as 3 inches in diameter) compared to the more typical L-head arrangement (both valves in the block on the same side of the cylinders) used by most manufacturers before World War II, but its combustion chambers were not efficient at all. Before the '20s, pre-detonation—knocking and pinging to you—was a common problem among most engines, especially those driven hard and fast. The T-head was especially susceptible to this malady.

Part of the problem also involved the poor gasoline used in those years. With only about 50 octane, those early fuels meant compression ratios had to stay quite low, say in the 4:1 neighborhood. Even at that low level, knocking and pinging was still a major problem.

A solution to this problem came in two forms. First, Britain's Harry Ricardo in 1922 successfully designed a "squish"-type combustion chamber that created turbulence in the air-fuel mixture as it was compressed. This turbulence greatly improved combustion efficiency and reduced the tendency for the fuel to pre-detonate due to inherent hot spots, such as around the exhaust valve. It worked; the Ricardo chamber allowed compression as high as 4.5:1, even with the existing bad gas. Chrysler wasted little time taking advantage of the design, using it on its new L-head six-cylinder in 1924. Many other L-heads from various marques soon appeared with similar combustion-chamber layouts.

High-Octane Fuels

The second half of the solution involved improved fuels. In 1923, GM researchers Charles "Boss" Kettering and Thomas Midgley, Jr., discovered tetraethyl lead, an additive that when mixed with standard gasoline could greatly increase octane. Three cubic centimeters in a gallon of gasoline instantly bumped up 55-octane gas by 15 octane points. This in turn meant compression ratios could jump above the then-unheard-of 6:1 level. By the end of 1923, GM's newly formed Ethyl Division was selling this additive in limited quantities in Ohio. Some five years later, "ethyl" gasoline could be found in filling stations across the country. Chrysler again took advantage of the situation, introducing its optional "Red Head" engine with 6.2:1 compression in 1928. Later, immediately following World War

II, Kettering's research team would experiment with a six-cylinder overhead-valve engine with a molecule-mashing 12.5:1 compression running on aviation-fuel-like 100-octane gasoline.

Engines Advances

Overhead valves had begun appearing more frequently in the '20s, although it was probably a mundane L-head design that drew the most attention in the decades leading up to World War II. In 1932, Henry Ford was again in the news, this time with his company's first V-8, the familiar "flathead." Despite its typically inefficient valve-in-block design, Ford's flathead V-8 was the perfect engine for the low-priced Model A; it was cheap to build and equally cheap to buy. It was also "peppy." Putting the 65-horsepower flathead into the '32 Model A weighing roughly 2500 pounds resulted in a relatively quick ride the common man could afford. Top speed was around 80 miles per hour and 0–60 miles per hour took about 18 seconds. Suddenly John Q. Public could outrun many so-called sporty machines costing much, much more than his "little Deuce coupe."

And with a little help from the quickly burgeoning performance aftermarket, the Ford flathead could, like its four-cylinder forerunners from Dearborn in the teens and '20s, be "hopped up" in a hurry. Easy to work on and readily available, thanks to the great number Ford rolled out in the '30s and '40s, the flathead V-8 quickly become the engine of choice for both racers and hot rodders alike. It would survive, however obsolete, up through 1953.

Among the flathead's more attractive characteristics was its compact "V" layout and its noticeably short stroke. All early engines had used very long strokes, basically to produce as much displacement as possible from four- or six-cylinder inline engines with slight bores. Bore size was limited because these inline engines had to fit beneath a car's hood—too big a bore diameter and an engine would've simply been too long. Cadillac first tried a more logical V-8 layout in 1914, Oldsmobile the following year, each not quite garnering the respect they deserved. At first. The obvious advantages of this arrangement, concerning both size and smoothness of operation, would become reborn soon enough, especially after Henry trotted out his version.

In the days of limited knowledge and technology around World War I, the easiest way to produce the most power was by squeezing it out of the most cubic inches possible. Even though some engine displacements before 1920 soared beyond 400 cubic inches, top outputs generally never even reached 100 horsepower. And this power was most often produced at a loafing 2000 rpm or so. Crude lubrication systems and those soft, cast-in babbitt bearings made it impossible to rev much beyond that limit and come home alive.

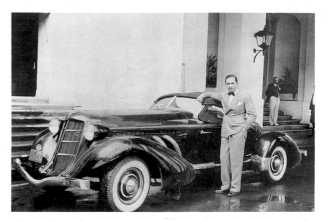

The Auburn-Cord-Duesenberg triumvirate lead the way in the '30s, both in price and performance. Even without optional supercharging, the top A-C-D sporty models were among the most powerful cars on American roads during the Depression years. And Auburn's "boat-tail" speedster was about as sexy as they came some 60 years ago.

A more desirable short-stroke design with its inherent high-winding capabilities would've never been possible in those days.

Some of the first steps towards higher rpm operation included the introduction of lightweight aluminum pistons and vibration dampers for the crankshaft, both features coming into being around 1915. Probably the next great advancement came in 1931 when Studebaker introduced the first steel-backed, insert-type bearings for the crank and connecting rods. These Clevite-produced inserts were more durable, more precise, and easier to replace than the old babbitt bearings. They could also endure greater bearing loads, meaning higher revs were then possible. Add the modern full-pressure lubrication systems then just coming into vogue and a whole new level of performance was made possible.

Such advancements aside, the basic rule in the '20s and '30s still remained "there's no substitute for cubic inches." Large, eight-cylinder inline engines became the rage in the '20s after Duesenberg introduced its straight-eight in 1921. Other new straight-eight rivals included Packard, Auburn, Jordan, Gardner, Elcar, and Stutz.

In the Duesenberg eight's case, size wasn't the only selling point. This particular straight-eight was indeed a "Duesie," what with its dual overhead high-lift/long-duration cams, aluminum pistons on tubular connecting rods, and four valves per cylinder. Displacing 420 cubic inches, the Duesenberg J eight was rated at 265 horsepower at 4200 rpm. Even more power was available once a gear-driven centrifugal supercharger was added. With five pounds of boost at 4000 rpm, this "blower" increased output to a definitely amazing 320 horses. Claims of a 120 miles per hour top end for the blown Duesenberg SJ—a car that weighed in

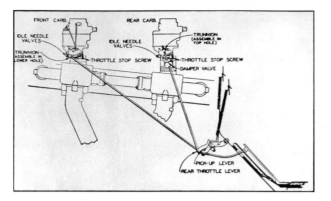

In 1941, Buick introduced this compound carburetor setup for its 320-cubic-inch straight-eight. Two Stromberg carbs were tied together by a progressive linkage that allowed only the front Stromberg to work during cruising. At upper rpm, the back carb kicked in to help produce 165 horsepower at 3800 revs. This design was the forerunner of the modern four-barrel carburetor.

at nearly two and a half tons—are believable. Its price at the time wasn't. SJ performance cost about $15,000 in the early '30s—a bunch of money today, literally a fortune back then.

To demonstrate just how high a big Duesenberg could fly, Augie Duesenberg and Ab Jenkins took the modified "Special" to the Bonneville Salt Flats in August 1935 for a shot at various speed records. Beneath the Special's streamlined body was a supercharged eight that reportedly put out 400 horsepower at 5000 rpm. With Jenkins driving, the car screamed to an unbelievable 152.145-mile-per-hour average for a 1-hour run, 135.47 miles per hour for 24 hours. Jenkins bought the Duesenberg Special after this performance, renaming it the *Mormon Meteor.* Over the following four years, he set even more records with his *Mormon Meteor* and raced it successfully in various match races.

Competing luxury makes trying to keep up with Duesenberg had begun turning to even bigger engines in the early '30s, with Lincoln and Packard choosing V-12s and Cadillac and Marmon going all the way up to massive V-16s. At a whopping 491 cubic inches, the famed Marmon V-16 produced 200 horsepower at 3400 rpm, enough oomph to move its three tons worth of high-class poshness with authority. Cadillac's V-16 was 452 cubic inches big and put out 165 maximum horses at 3400 rpm. In the V-12 ranks, Packard's powerplant measured 463 cubic inches and was rated at 175 horsepower at 3200 rpm. The smallest of this bunch was the Lincoln V-12, at 414 cubic inches. Maximum output was 150 horsepower at 3800 rpm.

Hands down, America's most powerful production cars of the '30s were the toys of the very rich. For just the plain rich—those not quite able to stomach 15, 10, or even 5 grand for an automobile—there were the

two other members of the Auburn-Cord-Duesenberg (A-C-D) triumvirate. Few sporty cars of the pre-war period could match the sexy lines of Auburn's boat-tail speedster, which also could've been equipped with a supercharged eight engine. Price was in the $2200 neighborhood. Beginning in 1929, the bigger Cords featured innovative front-wheel drive, and an optional supercharged engine became available for the stunning 812 model in 1937. A blown '37 Cord cost about twice as much as the Auburn.

Power for the Masses

Other than the "peppy" Model A, performance offerings aimed more at the masses were all but nonexistent during the Depression years. Probably the closest to this ideal was Hudson's straight-eight Terraplane of 1933 and '34. Like the V-8 Ford, this car combined light weight (less than 3000 pounds) and high power (92 horses) in a reasonably affordable package ($650). According to Hudson, the Terraplane-8 could run from 0 to 50 miles per hour in 13 seconds, 0 to 75 in eight clicks more.

For about $400–500 more, a speed-conscious customer in 1934 could've taken the wheel of yet another supercharged model, this one from Graham. Atop the company's 265-cubic-inch straight-eight, Graham's centrifugal supercharger—modeled after Duesenberg's—bumped output up from 95 horsepower to 135. Along with a 90mph top end (with overdrive), the blown Graham also offered uncharacteristically high fuel economy for a performance machine of its day—all this from a car that tipped the scales at around 3600 pounds.

Wearing a price tag comparable to the Graham, Buick's Century debuted in 1936, a combination of the big Roadmaster's 320-cubic-inch straight-eight engine and the lighter, smaller, cheaper Special's 118-inch-wheelbase chassis. Modern musclecar fans who think the GTO was the first car created by stuffing a big engine into a smaller car are mistaken. With 120 horses pulling about 3600 pounds, the Century quickly established itself in the late '30s as one of Detroit's better performance buys, a label it would continue wearing up through the '50s.

And, as if the Series 60 Century wasn't hot enough on its own, Buick engineers in 1941 added Detroit's first "compound-carburetor" setup as standard equipment. Optional for the Series 40 Specials, the Century's new induction equipment consisted of two Stromberg downdraft two-barrel carburetors, connected by a progressive linkage, on a special dual-plane, 180-degree intake manifold. Only the front two-barrel fed fuel/air to the straight eight during normal driving. But at about 75 miles per hour, the rear Stromberg would start waking up, eventually doubling the flow at full throttle. Sound familiar? Buick's compound carburetor arrangement was the precursor to the modern four-barrel carburetor, which later began appearing on optional performance engines in the early '50s.

Advancements like these from Buick represented one of many made by GM before the second World War. Among the more notable was Charles Kettering's electric starter (the first of Detroit's so-called "three most important automotive convenience devices"), introduced by Cadillac in 1912. In 1927, GM essentially became the industry's styling leader overnight, thanks to the creation of Detroit's first "in-house" styling department, the Art and Colour Section, headed by the legendary Harley Earl.

Seven years later, Buick, Oldsmobile, and Cadillac pioneered the basic independent-front-suspension layout that quickly became the rule among American chassis designs. In place of the solid "beam" axles (suspended by longitudinal leaf springs) used before 1934, GM's "knee-action" design featured coil springs sandwiched between parallel, lateral "A-arms," the forerunner of today's SLA (short-arm/long-arm) front suspensions. Buick, in 1938, even went to coil springs for its rear suspension.

Automatic Transmissions

The second of the "three most important automotive convenience devices" (number three, power steering, came later via Chrysler in 1951) was also a GM innovation. On September 24, 1939, Oldsmobile announced a new $57 option for its 1940 models. That feature was the Hydra-Matic automatic transmission. Although not the first of its breed—various automatic transmission experiments had been tried dating back almost to the birth of the automobile—GM's Hydra-Matic easily was, at the time, the most successful, best accepted variation on the automatic transmission theme. Previously, the best-working "shiftless" transmissions had been of the "semi-automatic" type—a clutch was required for starts, but from there gear changes were automatic. Reo is credited with the first truly successful semi-automatic in 1933, and Oldsmobile introduced another in 1937, followed by Buick in 1938.

The Hydra-Matic, however, was fully automatic, with fluid coupling taking the place of a conventional clutch. Although semi-automatics did survive into the early '50s (courtesy of Chrysler Corporation), once the Olds transmission arrived, rival automakers quickly began jumping on the automatic bandwagon. Buick introduced its Dynaflow in 1948, the same year Pontiac picked up the Hydra-Matic. And Packard first offered its Ultramatic in 1949. By 1951, automatics were in, and shifting by hand was slowly becoming old news.

The Modern V-8

Perhaps the greatest GM innovation, from a performance perspective, came a few years before, courtesy of Boss Kettering's experiments with high-octane fuels and ultra-high-compression engines. On November 3, 1948, production of Oldsmobile's famed "Rocket" engine commenced, kicking off the era of the truly modern V-8. Developed concurrently with the Olds Rocket, a Cadillac counterpart appeared two months later in January 1949. Both were high-winding, short-stroke mills with overhead valves and state-of-the-art high compression, 7.5:1 for the Cadillac, 7.25:1 for the Olds. Though it was commonly referred to as the "Kettering engine," the 303-cubic-inch Rocket V-8 was chiefly the work of engineer Gilbert Burrell. John Gordon, Harry Barr, and Ed Cole contributed to the development of Cadillac's 331-cubic-inch overhead-valve V-8.

Plain and simple, it was these two thoroughly modern V-8s that kicked off the great American horsepower race. Maximum output for the Olds Rocket was listed as 135 horsepower at 3600 rpm. Producing 160 horses at 3800 rpm, Cadillac's hot new V-8 put it at the head of the horsepower pack running into the '50s.

But it wasn't long before the rest of the pack started cutting into that lead as the '50s performance market began taking shape. As the decade took off, so, too, did the high-powered American automobile.

Preston Tucker with his ill-fated "Torpedo" in 1948. With its extremely low, aerodynamic body and a big, rear-mounted six-cylinder engine, the '48 Tucker could easily surpass 100 miles per hour. Had Tucker's dream machine gone onto regular production, it would have, without a doubt, helped redefine the way Americans looked at performance. But various pitfalls—economical and political—closed down the Chicago automaker after only 51 cars were built.

NEW AND IMPROVED
Engineering and Design Advances

NO ifs, ands, or buts about it, the key to the development of American performance in the '50s was the arrival of the high-compression, short-stroke, overhead-valve V-8. Like Ford's long-running "flathead" L-head V-8, GM's much-more-modern, much-more-powerful overhead-valve V-8s, introduced for '49 Oldsmobiles and Cadillacs, were compact and well-balanced. And that compactness not only meant these engines would fit easily beneath any hood, it also meant their displacement growth potential was great; in the absence of any other performance advancements, the easiest way to pull more horsepower from any engine is by increasing cubic inches.

The way those cubic inches were derived also had a lot to do with the decade's rapid performance growth. Displacement is a function of bore and stroke; increasing both of these factors at the same time or either one while keeping the other constant, by physical law, always has and always will translate into more cubic inches. But there are drawbacks to simply enlarging either half of the "bore-times-stroke" equation. In the pre-war era when inline engines dominated the scene, only so much bore diameter could be incorporated before total cylinder-block length went beyond typical engine-compartment parameters—too large a bore, multiplied by however many cylinders were involved, translated into too long a

cylinder block to fit behind most radiators. Consequently, all early inline engines used longer strokes to derive more displacement from small-bore blocks.

Short-Stroke Design

While long-stroke engines deliver loads of torque—just what early automakers needed to move heavy cars up hills with low horsepower engines—the downside of a long stroke is excessive piston travel and too much "lateral" connecting rod motion. This means more friction, which both shortens engine life (due to quicker wear) and inhibits higher rpm operation. Long-stroke engines are inherently low-rpm luggers; various physical laws see to that.

Short strokes, on the other hand, mean less wear since all parts involved are moving around less through the reciprocating process, at least during normal, everyday operation. And since the reciprocating mass (crankshaft, rods, pistons, and so on) has not as far to go as the crank spins around, it can do this dance with far less sweat, meaning much higher rotational speeds are possible. Short-stroke engines are naturally high winders, limited only by their overall ability to rapidly pump air and hold everything together at extremely high revs.

Additionally, GM's new short-stroke V-8s were of the "over-square" variety—that is, bore diameter measured greater than stroke length. Conversely, long-stroke engines with small bore diameters are considered "under-square." Even with its relatively short stroke, Ford's venerable, small-displacement flathead V-8 was under-square, its 239-cubic-inch version of 1948 featuring a meager 3.19-inch bore and 3.75-inch stroke. These two terms are derived from the measurement of an engine's bore-to-stroke ratio.

Discounting the exorbitantly priced, rarely seen supercharged Duesenbergs of the '30s, the first "regular production" car out of Detroit to feature 300 horsepower was Chrysler's original letter-series model, introduced in 1955. Beneath the hood of the beautiful C300 was Chrysler's 300-horsepower, 331-cubic-inch Firepower V-8.

Thanks to its relative light weight and powerful Rocket V-8, Oldsmobile's 88 probably stands as America's first modern performance car. Early domination of NASCAR stock car racing helped support this claim. This Olds is a '50 Holiday coupe.

General Motors set the early pace in Detroit's horsepower race, introducing modern overhead-valve V-8s for both Cadillac and Oldsmobile in 1949. The smaller of the two, Oldsmobile's Rocket V-8 displaced 303 cubic inches and churned out 135 maximum horses at 3600 rpm. The big, oil-bath air cleaner appearing here was an option in 1950; a typical dry-element filter was standard.

As in example, Cadillac's previously used 346-cubic-inch L-head V-8 featured a bore-to-stroke ratio of 0.78:1, compared to 1.05:1 for its 1949 replacement, the 331-cubic-inch overhead-valve V-8. A ratio greater than 1:1 (the latter) is over-square, less than 1:1 (the former) is under-square.

GM's engineers obviously had to turn to the over-square layout to produce the desired engine displacement while using a shorter stroke. And since the compact "V" layout fit so snuggly between radiator and cowl, increasing bore diameter was no longer as much a worry as before. Coincidentally, increasing bore also translated into more room in the combustion chamber for the valves, which were now located directly overhead instead of within the block to the side of each cylinder, per the old L-head specifications. With extra room inside the cylinder, larger-diameter valves could be installed, resulting in increased "breathing" and higher horsepower potential.

Better breathing and a serious increase in volumetric efficiency—how well the fuel-air charge is combusted—represented the most important improvements inherent to the overhead-valve design. L-heads, by nature, were notoriously bad breathers, since the fuel-air mixture and spent gases had to follow such an inhibited, circuitous route in and out of the combustion-chamber/cylinder arena, which, as you may have guessed, was shaped like an inverted "L" from a longitudinal perspective. Overhead valves, however, allowed much smoother passages into and out of a combustion chamber that was located fully atop the cylinder—no sideways extension areas were present to complicate efficient flame propagation and limit compression increases, as was the case with an L-head engine.

The overhead-valve layout let engineers design much more efficient combustion chambers where flame travel could be evened out more precisely and compression levels could be increased beyond previously limited L-head standards. While Cadillac's L-head and overhead-valve V-8s of 1948 and 1949, respectively, both featured then-high compression levels—7.25:1 for the former, 7.5:1 for the latter—the potential for even higher ratios for the overhead-valve engine in years to come was promising. Not nearly so for the L-head.

If there was a negative aspect of the overhead-valve layout, it involved the plain fact that this design added more moving parts (primarily rocker arms atop the cylinder heads) compared to valve-in-block engines, thus injecting unwanted weight into the reciprocating-mass equation. The more weight, the tougher it is to convince that mass to reciprocate at higher rpm. And speaking of weight, obviously the overhead-valve cylinder heads themselves were heavier than their L-head counterparts, which were no more than thin, flat (thus the Ford nickname "flathead"), iron cylinder covers with combustion chambers carved into them.

All things being equal, these aspects would've represented a downside for the overhead-valve design. But things weren't anywhere near equal in the case of GM's modern overhead-valve V-8. Its relative compactness and increased power potential from less displacement meant it could be engineered much smaller and lighter than its valve-in-block predecessor. And its short stroke and relatively lightweight valvetrain ensured that rpm limits could go where no L-head had gone before.

GM Takes an Early Lead

Armed with such weaponry, GM of course took the early lead in the postwar horsepower race as

Along with being lauded as *Motor Trend*'s "Car of the Year," Chrysler's new Firepower V-8 model for 1951 was also chosen as the prestigious pace car for the Indianapolis 500. *Courtesy Chrysler Historical*

Cadillac's 160-horsepower 331-cubic-inch overhead-valve V-8 jumped first out of the gate. Naturally, Cadillacs of the early '50s were the recognized "hot cars" of the day, what with impressive speed potential—100 miles per hour was possible—coupled with all that luxury, class, and "coolness." The latter aspect primarily came by way of cutting-edge styling featuring the industry's first tailfins, added per Harley Earl's direction in 1948.

But the status-laden Cadillacs typically carried heavy price tags, every bit as heavy as the cars themselves. Oldsmobiles, on the other hand, were as much as a grand cheaper and 300 or 400 pounds lighter in 1949. Thanks to its lighter stance, the Olds was an able performer, even with its smaller 135-horsepower 303-cubic-inch overhead-valve V-8. Its power-to-weight ratio was probably the best in the industry at the time, and its ability to accelerate from rest to 60 miles per hour in about 12 seconds was also on the cutting edge. So it was that, by 1950, the Olds Rocket 88 coupe was best recognized by the masses as a true performance machine—arguably the first of the modern postwar era. Any doubts were quickly squelched once the Rocket 88 started kicking butt and taking names on the fledgling National Association of Stock Car Auto Racing (NASCAR) stock-car circuit.

With the overhead-valve gauntlet laid down by Oldsmobile and Cadillac, rival automakers had no choice but to develop high-powered counterparts of

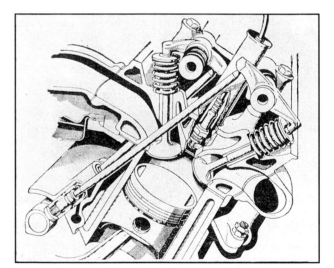

Chrysler's innovative Firepower V-8 relied on a potent cylinder head design featuring, among other things, hemispherical combustion chambers—thus the nickname "hemi." This technical drawing depicts Dodge's version, which first appeared in 1953.

their own or continue eating dust. As it turned out, the modern high-compression overhead-valve V-8 not only ended up being the tool by which the men were separated from the boys in the early '50s performance game, it also became one of the main keys to ultimate survival in the decade's rapidly changing, increasingly competitive market.

26

Chrysler was next among the fully entrenched "Big Three" to unveil an all-new overhead-valve V-8, it coming in 1951. DeSoto followed suit in 1952 and Dodge in 1953. Plymouth's first wouldn't come until 1955, the same year GM's lowest-price divisions, Chevrolet and Pontiac, introduced theirs. Buick, the '40s performance leader, finally traded its yeoman overhead-valve straight-eight for an overhead-valve V-8 in 1953.

For Ford Motor Company, Lincoln led the way into the modern horsepower race with its first overhead-valve V-8 in 1952. Both Mercury and Ford finally gave up on Henry's old flathead after 1953, reappearing with varying renditions of Dearborn's "Y-block" overhead-valve V-8 the following year. As for the rest, it had become painfully clear by the early '50s that a so-called "independent" automaker either had to run with the big dogs and their modern V-8s, or stay on the porch with his antiquated L-head and rock away into retirement.

Packard's eventual demise, coming in July 1958, can be traced to its inability to quickly catch up, power-wise, in the postwar luxury field. The once-proud marque didn't introduce its first overhead-valve V-8 until 1955. Packard's partner by mid-decade, Studebaker initially managed to hang tough in the years immediately following the war thanks to an early jump in the industry's thoroughly modern styling competition and the arrival of an up-to-date overhead-valve V-8 in 1951. But such advancements came at a cost the century-old independent firm from South Bend, Indiana, couldn't quite pay, thus the buy-out by Packard in June 1954. Kaiser-Frazer and Willys never did rise above the antiquated L-head stage of evolution. This fact, along with various other contributing factors, helped bring about their disappearance from the American market after 1955.

Nash-Kelvinator bought its first V-8 from Packard in 1955, sharing that overhead-valve engine with its corporate cousin Hudson, which had merged with Nash to form the American Motors Corporation (AMC) in April 1954. Economy-conscious Nash had done well enough before the merger with its overhead-valve inline six-cylinder. This was a nicely efficient, reasonably potent powerplant that by 1954 had the industry's second highest compression level at 8.5:1—Packard's 212-horsepower L-head straight-eight led the way at 8.7:1. But even more impressive was what Hudson designers had accomplished prior to 1954 using the cards they had been dealt.

Hudson and NASCAR

Like Studebaker, Hudson had been quick to offer totally fresh styling to postwar buyers, introducing its innovative "stepdown" bodyshell in 1948. Wearing trend-setting slabside sheetmetal on the outside, the

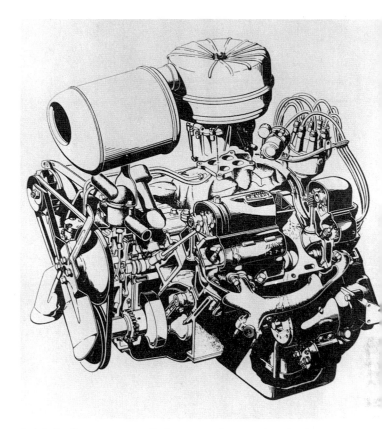

Buick finally gave up on its long-running overhead-valve straight-eight in 1953, trading it for this overhead-vavle V-8. Fed by a Carter four-barrel carburetor, Buick's 322-cubic-inch V-8 produced 188 horsepower beneath a '53 Roadmaster's hood.

stepdown Hudson underneath featured unitized body-chassis construction with widely spaced perimeter frame rails running outside the rear wheels. This unique design also allowed the interior compartment floor to run low and wide between those rails, meaning passengers had to step down when entering.

That low floor, in turn, meant the roofline could be dropped without reducing headroom, resulting in a car that was as long, low, and sleek as anything then on American roads. The performance potential of Hudson's rigid, sure-footed, relatively aerodynamic stepdown shell quickly became clear, especially to professional hot-foots who wasted little time putting early '50s Hudsons at the head of the NASCAR racing pack. On the young NASCAR circuit, the Hudson Hornet was soon the "Fabulous Hudson Hornet."

Almost amazingly, this racing success came without state-of-the-art overhead valves. Or eight cylinders. Or even a V. Powering those fabulous Hornets was Hudson's reliable straight-six, a valve-in-block L-head engine, albeit a very large one. Introduced at 262 cubic inches in 1948, the durable, brawny Hudson flathead six was expanded to a healthy 308 cubic inches and 145 horsepower in 1951, the year Herb Thomas drove a

Innovative was a fair description for Nash models in the '50s, what with their trend-setting unit-body construction and definitely different Pinin Farina sheetmetal. Beneath the hood of this '54 Ambassador coupe is Nash's hottest powerplant, the Dual Jetfire Le Mans six-cylinder.

Hornet to a NASCAR seasonal points championship for the first time. With additional accomplished drivers such as Marshall Teague, Tim Flock, Frank Mundy, and Dick Rathmann at their wheels, Hudsons would go on to dominate the stock-car scene up through 1954, the last year for the stepdown Hornet.

That big, bullet-proof six, combined with the stepdown body's low center of gravity, were the prime factors behind Hudson's NASCAR domi-

nance. According to Hudson brochures, the 308 six's "extreme ruggedness" helped explain how this pre-war throwback managed to survive so well in a highly competitive postwar world full of cutting-edge V-8s. Continued the brochure: "The oversize bearings, the extreme rigidity and hardness of the block, the weight and stiffness of the crankshaft—in fact the extra sturdiness built into all parts—make it possible to utilize . . . extra power."

The man who first helped make it possible for Herb Thomas' Hornets to win with relative ease was none other than ace racing mechanic Henry "Smokey" Yunick, long-time proprietor of Daytona Beach's "best damn garage in town," and the same man who would later in the decade work similar competition-minded magic for Chevrolet and Pontiac. Yunick's main man at Hudson in those heady race-winning days of the early '50s was a young engineer named Vince Piggins, who himself would end up working for Chevrolet, as well, once Hudson faded from the scene. At Chevrolet, Piggins went on to oversee that division's performance-parts development projects. Later feathers in his cap would include the various exotic "COPO" cars, the most prominent being the all-aluminum ZL-1 Camaro and the rarely seen 427 Chevelle, both of 1969.

At Hudson in 1952, Piggins was put in charge of the company's "severe-usage parts program," a direct response to the challenges presented by the rigorous—make that torturous—NASCAR competition. The promotional opportunities that stock-car competition offered had not been lost on company officials. In a September 1952 meeting, Hudson parts merchandising manager H. L. Templin was among the first to speak loudly of the possibilities, describing "the great value Hudson has obtained from stock-car racing." He continued: "The publicity covering Hudson's many wins has been of untold benefit to us." As much as Templin pressed for complete dealer familiarity with the company's severe-usage parts project, it would for the most part remain a low-key operation.

Nonetheless it was a successful one.

At the time, stock-car racing was, by decree, intended only for "stock cars," a breed that seemingly was being redefined by the race as "cheaters" continually created their own definition of "factory stock." By officially opening its severe-usage parts counter for business, Hudson made things completely legal per NASCAR mandates—these race-ready parts were available from the factory as stock parts so they were legal for stock-car competition. Not since the record-setting Duesenbergs of the mid-1930s had a major American automaker involved itself so fully in a factory-backed high-speed project. And never before had such involvement also resulted in such a prominent performance enhancement aimed at the everyday driver.

That enhancement was "Twin H-Power," an optional dual-carburetor induction setup that helped boost the big six's output to 160 horsepower. According to Hudson's hype-masters, "the secret of the amazing results which Twin H-Power provides is that it so accurately measures gasoline, so evenly distributes it to each cylinder, and so thoroughly vaporizes the fuel with air that it provides what the engineers call far better 'breathing' and combustion than

A relatively potent engine (for an efficient six-cylinder) in its standard state, Nash's 252-cubic-inch, overhead-valve six was bumped up to 140 healthy horses thanks to the addition of two Carter sidedraft carburetors and an increase to 8:1 compression. The two small open-element air cleaners shown here are not stock.

has heretofore been obtainable. Most important, this greatly improved efficiency is obtained on regular grade gasoline. There is no need to pay for premium grade fuels. [Twin H-Power] provides jet-like pickup and a sustained flow of terrific energy. [And it] gives you stepped-up power where you need it most, in the ordinary driving range."

At the same time, a whole host of stepped-up parts began trickling out of Piggins' department. Early NASCAR races had demonstrated that stock steel

Nash automobiles of the '50s could have been considered "hot cars" even without the twin-carb Le Mans six-cylinder. Innovation also carried over inside, where fold-down front seats quickly transformed the passenger compartment into a bedroom. Watching the submarine races would never be the same again.

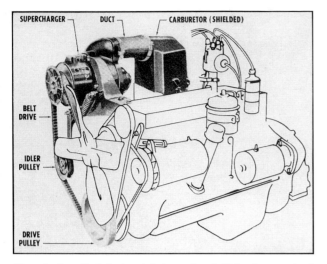

One factor that helped bring about Kaiser's eventual downfall was its inability to develop a modern, overhead-valve V-8 of its own. Instead, Kaiser-Willys opted for supercharged power in 1954. Standard for Manhattan models, Kaiser's blown 226-cubic-inch six-cylinder featured a McCulloch-supplied centrifugal supercharger, which upped output to 140 horsepower.

wheels were factory cars' weakest link, coming apart easily when stressed. And when racers reinforced their wheels themselves, spindles tended to break. Piggins' men responded by working with the Kelsey-Hayes company to develop the industry's first heavy-duty, race-ready rim. Offered as well were spindles and steering arms that were shot-peened for extra strength. Beefy, large-diameter rear axles, strengthened hubs with bigger bolts, stiffer shock absorbers, dual exhaust kits, an "extra high-performance" cam, a heavy-duty radiator, an extra-capacity fuel tank, high-compression heads—the list was as impressive as it was long.

Late in 1953, Hudson also introduced the "7X" racing option for the 308 six-cylinder. Officially announced in August primarily as a short-block replacement-engine package, the $385 7X engine featured an overbored block that was "plunge cut" into the cylinders to unshroud the valves. Inside went a high-lift cam, and a high-compression head went on top, held down by studs drilled into the block. Twin H-Power was included, as was a special split exhaust manifold. Common estimates put output for the 7X six-cylinder at 210 horsepower. Very few were sold.

In 1954, some of the tricks tried with the 7X package were extended to the regular-production line. Hudson's six was fitted with a lumpier cam and an aluminum high-compression (7.5:1) head, which upped output to 160 horses, 170 with optional Twin H-Power. In terms of horsepower per cubic inch, the Twin H-Power Hudson in 1954 ranked right up at the

top, along with Detroit's various overhead-valve V-8s. That honor served as a suitable send-off for the Fabulous Hornet—the very last stepdown Hudson rolled off the line at the company's old Jefferson Avenue plant in Detroit on October 29, 1954. Beginning in 1955, Hudsons became glorified Nash models built right alongside their corporate cousins in Kenosha, Wisconsin.

Nash already had a few things in common with Hudson, even before the AMC merger of 1954. Like the stepdowns had, the new Nash for 1950 featured innovative lightweight-yet-sturdy unit-body construction. And Nash also offered a performance-minded six-cylinder with twin carburetors in the '50s. This engine, too, was inspired by competition endeavors.

In December 1949, Nash-Kelvinator's George Mason and British sports-car racer Donald Healey met and decided to build an English-American hybrid featuring a Healey-built sporting chassis and Nash's new overhead-valve six-cylinder, then just entering production for 1950. Right out of the box, the Nash 234-cubic-inch six produced 112 horsepower. Healey bettered that by adding an aluminum high-compression (8:1) head, a hot cam, and two British SU carburetors on a special intake. The resulting 125-horsepower Nash-Healey sports-car prototypes, wearing makeshift bodies, quickly demonstrated their worth as one was driven to a fourth-place overall finish at Le Mans in 1950. Another Nash-Healey claimed sixth overall at the 24-hour endurance classic in 1951, followed by third-place honors the following year. Back in America, 506 regular-production Nash-Healeys were built from 1951 to 1954, with some leftover coupes ending up being sold as 1955 models.

Just as Hudson's people had put the Fabulous Hornets' NASCAR successes to good use as a promotional tool, so, too, were Mason's men at Nash more than willing to use some of those French laurels to boost

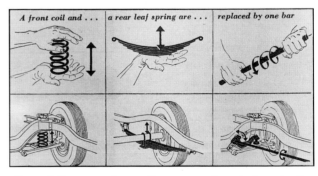

One of the more innovative suspension designs in the '50s came from Packard, which in 1955 introduced its intriguing torsion-bar chassis. Two long torsion bars tied front and rear wheels together, supposedly helping the car "step over" bumps and jolts more effectively than typical coil or leaf springs.

Like Nash, Hudson had also tried unitized body construction, introducing its so-called "stepdown" models in 1948. With its exceptionally low center of gravity and widely spaced perimeter frame rails running outside the rear wheels, the stepdown Hudsons proved to be formidable forces in stock car racing. Many consider the '54 Hornet to be the best-looking of the stepdown breed.

While other automakers were turning to overhead-valve powerplants in the early '50s, Hudson continued to rely on its large L-head six-cylinder flathead engine. And with optional Twin-H Power, the dual-carb Hudson six was certainly no slouch, as NASCAR competitors soon discovered. In 1954, Hudson's 308-cubic-inch Twin-H Power engine was rated at 170 horsepower.

their cars' image here in America. In 1953, they introduced the Le Mans Dual Jetfire engine as an option for their Ambassador series, which, along with its lesser-priced Statesman running mate, had been adorned with a new Pinin Farina-styled body in 1952. With two Carter side-draft carburetors controlled by a progressive linkage, the enlarged 252-cubic-inch overhead-valve Dual Jetfire six-cylinder produced 140 horsepower at 4000 rpm, 20 more horses than the standard single-Carter six. Ambassadors equipped with the Dual Jetfire six also received a small "Le Mans" emblem on each rear quarterpanel. Nash's Le Mans Dual Jetfire option returned in identical form one more time in 1954 before falling by the wayside once an overhead-valve V-8 debuted under Ambassador hoods the following year.

Along with the Hudson and Nash engines, a third multi-carb six-cylinder had also debuted in 1953, this one from Chevrolet for its exciting, new Corvette. Fed by three Carter side-draft one-barrel carburetors, the Corvette's Blue Flame six produced 150 horses, more than enough to instantly make the ground-breaking fiberglass two-seater one of this country's quickest production cars.

The Hemi Takes Over

As for additional V-8 advancements, the second most important introduction after GM's in 1949, had come by way of Chrysler in 1951. If horsepower race fans thought the Cadillac and Oldsmobile V-8s were hot, they had another thing coming once Chrysler's famed Firepower V-8 arrived that year. Like its GM rivals, the Firepower engine featured a short stroke (3.625 inches, same as Cadillac's), high compression (7.5:1), and overhead valves. It displaced 331 cubic inches, again, the same as Cadillac. From there, however, comparisons faded.

Dating back to development work first considered in 1935, the Firepower V-8 used unique overhead-valve heads featuring hemispherical combustion chambers, centrally located spark plugs, and inclined valves on dual rocker shafts. It was that combustion-chamber's shape that soon led to this innovative engine's nickname—"hemi." Hemi heads were not necessarily anything new at the time; the design could be traced back to 1904, with later renditions coming in various World War I aircraft, sporting machines from Duesenberg and Stutz, racers from Miller and

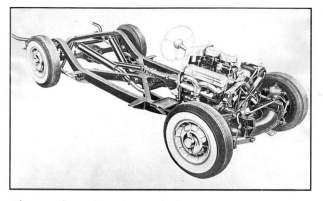

After Nash and Hudson's dual-carburetor six-cylinders came various twin-carb V-8s from Cadillac, Packard, and Chrysler beginning in 1955. In 1956, Chevrolet also introduced dual four-barrels for both the Corvette and the passenger-car line. This is the '56 Corvette chassis fitted with its 225-horsepower, 265-cubic-inch V-8 fed by a pair of Carter four-barrel carburetors.

Offenhauser, and Jaguar's XK120 of 1949. But no automaker to that point had used the hemi head so effectively—in mass-produced fashion to boot—as Chrysler did beginning in 1951.

The advantages of the hemi-head design were many. First, the symmetrical, "domed" combustion chambers, with their spark plugs mounted smack dab in the center, offered superb volumetric efficiency as flame propagation was as near perfect as possible. The physical aspect of that chamber also meant there was more room for bigger valves compared to GM's "wedge"-shaped design. And since those valves were inclined to match the curve of the hemi chamber, they allowed straighter, less-restrictive passage for both intake and exhaust flow. Hemi ports didn't "bend" as much as their wedge-head counterparts'—the intake valves angled up to match their corresponding ports and the exhaust valves did so identically in the opposite direction to the same effect. In with the good air, out with the bad was simply a breeze for the Firepower V-8, far more so than for any rival overhead-valve V-8.

Additionally, with those inclined valves opening up at an angle away from the cylinder wall into the combustion chamber, "shrouding" wasn't a problem. Nor were the "hot spots" typically created in other engines when the cool intake fuel/air charge encountered the hotter exhaust valve area too quickly. Wedge heads inherently suffer some form of valve shrouding, that is flow restriction caused where the valve comes closest to the cylinder wall. Hemi valves basically worked far apart in comparatively wide-open spaces, meaning hot spots were minimized and breathing was nothing short of sensational, head and shoulders above anything else offered in the '50s. Or the '60s and '70s for that matter.

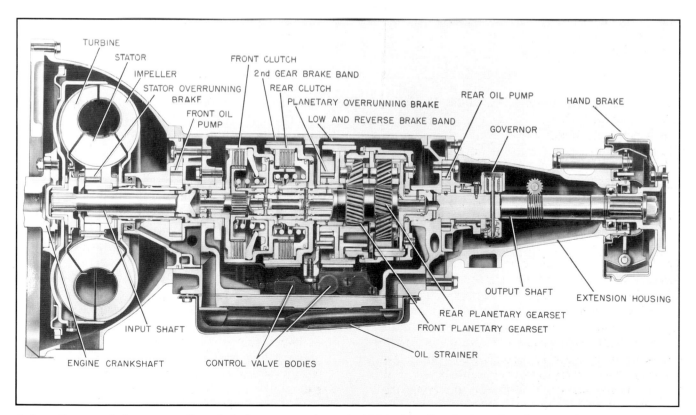

Automatic transmissions were still a relatively new experiment in 1956 when Chrysler introduced its superb Torqueflite three-speed automatic for the 300B luxury cruiser. A marked improvement over Chrysler's existing two-speed Powerflite transmission, born late in 1953, the tough Torqueflite became an option for all Chryslers in 1957.

Chevrolet's Ramjet fuel-injection option debuted in 1957, most prominently beneath the Corvette's fiberglass hood. The Rochester-supplied "fuelie" setup was also available for any passenger-line model. Here, chief Corvette engineer Zora Arkus-Duntov (right) shows off his work to veteran *Mechanix Illustrated* scribe "Uncle" Tom McCahill. *Courtesy Noland Adams*

Yet another advantage involved the way the hemi head dealt with high compression ratios. As Chrysler's Engineering and Research director, James Zeder, explained in a 1951 Society of Automotive Engineers (SAE) paper, "at 7.5:1 compression, [the Firepower V-8] does not require the high-cost, premium grades of fuel which must be used in other conventional overhead valve V-8 engines at the same compression ratio." Superb volumetric efficiency, combined with the near total absence of combustion-chamber hot spots, contributed to the hemi engine's apparent immunity to pre-detonation, even with industry-leading compression ratios.

The downside to the hemi design involved its complex valvetrain and overall mass and weight. Twin rocker shafts were needed to locate the inclined valves. And while the heads themselves were interchangeable side to side, the rocker arms and pushrods—from the

intake side to exhaust—were not. They varied considerably in order to work with the parallel rocker shafts. Predictably, hemi heads were extremely large as well, making for a tight fit between most fenders on '50s Chrysler products. Coincidentally, these large chunks of cast-iron were quite heavy; a pair in 1951 weighed 120 pounds, compared to a relatively svelte 94 pounds for Cadillac's wedge heads.

Any and all negative aspects, however, were quickly left behind once a driver in 1951 began putting his right foot into the Firepower V-8, offered along with the luxurious New Yorker and the less costly Saratoga. Available for use at his discretion were 180 horses found at 4000 rpm. Maximum torque of 312 pounds-feet arrived at 2000 rpm. Measuring 6 inches shorter between its wheels compared to the New Yorker, and weighing some 250 pounds less, the revamped '51 Saratoga was the prime choice for a

Chrysler customer wanting to show a Cadillac driver a thing or two that year.

On paper, the hemi-powered Chrysler had already sped past Cadillac in Detroit's horsepower race, its industry-leading 180-horsepower output topping GM's luxury liner by 20 horses. On the road, it was also no contest; according to a startling *Road & Track* road test, the 3,948-pound hemi Saratoga could hit 60 miles per hour from rest in only 10 seconds, seemingly a violation of physical laws. At least in some states.

"*Road & Track*'s test crew seldom gets excited about American cars," claimed the review, "but then *Road & Track*'s readers are familiar with this attitude. The Chrysler is an exception. While it has faults, and some of them are serious, we feel that it is outstanding among local efforts." In conclusion, the *Road & Track* report claimed "the tremendous performance of this V-8 is enough in itself to be a strong selling point for the Chrysler. Regardless of the rest of the car's advantages or disadvantages, when you touch that throttle, you know something mighty impressive is happening under the hood."

Motor Trend's editors were so impressed they named the new 1951 Firepower Chrysler "Car of the Year," the same honor they had extended to Cadillac in honor of its overhead-valve V-8 in 1949. According to *Motor Trend*'s Griffith Borgeson, the hemi-powered Chrysler in 1951 represented "a major step ahead in American automotive history."

While Cadillac jumped back into the horsepower lead in 1952 with its 190-horsepower 331-cubic-inch V-8, Chrysler's hemi remained the engine to beat on the street, where it also began appearing beneath DeSoto hoods in 160-horsepower, 276-cubic-inch, Firedome V-8 form. And when Dodge got its first overhead-valve V-8 in 1953, it was none other than a hemi. Dodge's version initially displaced 241 cubic inches and was rated at 140 horsepower. Various other sizes and outputs followed for Dodge and DeSoto over the years to come.

In 1954, Chrysler's 235-horsepower hemi put it back at the head of the horsepower pack following Cadillac's two-year run. Hemi power then went on to dominate the Detroit performance crowd up through 1957.

"Bigger is better" became the rule as the '50s progressed. In 1955, Packard's first modern overhead-valve engine, at 352 cubic inches, became Detroit's first postwar V-8 to cross the 350-cubic-inch threshold; the company's previously used L-head straight-eight, at 359 cubic inches, had crossed that threshold the year before. Packard again led the field in displacement the following year at 374 cubic inches. Then Chrysler's hemi soared from 354 cubes to 392 in 1957. In 1958, Ford Motor Company became the first to crash the 400-cubic-inch barrier as both Mercury and Lincoln rolled out massive 430-cubic-inch V-8s. The newborn Edsel's top V-8 measured 410 cubic inches that year.

Compression levels, too, began running sky high in the '50s. Engineers and customers alike early in the decade had considered 7.5:1 to be high compression. By 1954, Cadillac V-8 compression had risen to 8.25:1, Nash's aforementioned overhead-valve six-cylinder to 8.5:1, and Packard's big 359-cubic-inch straight-eight to 8.7:1. Then, in 1956, Chrysler's 300B could be equipped with an optional 354-cubic-inch hemi V-8 featuring head-popping 10:1 compression. The following year, the 283-horsepower Corvette upped the ante to 10.5:1. Reaching Boss Kettering's earlier experimental limits of 12.5:1 would have to wait until the '60s.

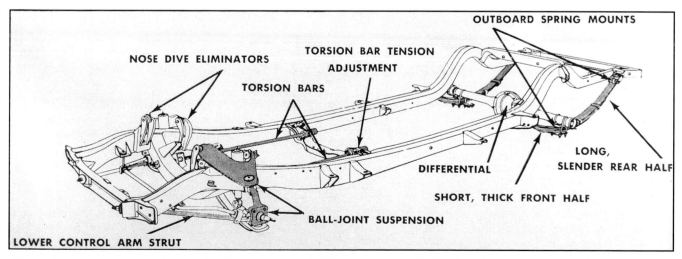

Although Packard began using torsion bars to suspend all four wheels in 1955, Chrysler engineers would not adapt torsion bars until 1957, and then only for the front wheels. Also new that year were outboard-mounted rear leaf springs which helped increase roll stiffness considerably. Overall, Chrysler's new 1957 chassis was probably Detroit's best as far as handling was concerned.

Triple carburetors debuted on the Corvette's Blue Flame six-cylinder engine in 1953. Four years later, both Oldsmobile and Pontiac engineers introduced tri-carb options—J-2 and Tri Power, respectively—for their top performance V-8s. Appearing here is Oldsmobile's 1958 J-2 setup. *Courtesy Oldsmobile Division, General Motors*

Output levels gained even more momentum after 1955, the year Chrysler cracked the 300-horsepower barrier. By 1958, at least 10 different V-8s were rated at more than 300 horsepower, with that 430-cube monster from Lincoln and Mercury leading the way as Detroit's first 400-horsepower engine. Chrysler's equally large 392-cubic-inch hemi was right behind at 390 horses.

Transmitting All That Power

Of course, to handle all that power, engineers had to also stay in step concerning transmission development. By the time the 400-horsepower Lincoln-Mercury V-8 was unleashed in 1958, transmission technology had developed to the point where Ford Motor Company engineers could even use an automatic transmission behind that 430-inch monster, a proposition that would have had them shuddering just a few years before. A Mercury buyer in 1958 could've

backed up his 400-horsepower 430 V-8 with a Multi-Matic automatic, a beefed-up, dual-range version of the Merc-O-Matic trans, Mercury's first automatic, introduced in 1951. According to *Motor Trend*'s Don Francisco, Mercury's Multi-Matic was "without a doubt, the best automatic transmission that has ever been available in any car."

Chrysler fans might've disagreed, as their favorite marque's Torqueflite, a thoroughly modern three-speed automatic introduced on the 1956 300B, was as tough as they came in the '50s. This automatic had to be able to handle the punishment put out by the 300's hemi V-8. The Torqueflite had superseded the less-impressive two-speed Powerflite transmission that had appeared as Chrysler's first automatic late in 1953.

Buick had had an automatic transmission since 1948, the smooth, yet sluggish Dynaflow. Called the "Dyna-slush" by critics, early Dynaflows didn't do much for Buick performance. But various upgrades later in the '50s would right that wrong. Much the same could be said for Chevrolet's two-speed Powerglide, which had debuted in 1950. Chevy wouldn't get a better performing auto trans until the Turboglide was unveiled in 1957.

Independent Studebaker brought out its first automatic, a three-speed box supplied by Borg-Warner, in 1951. That same year, Lincoln, Hudson, and Kaiser each turned to GM for their first automatic, the proven Hydra-Matic. Lincoln's own automatic, Turbo-Drive, debuted in 1955.

With few exceptions in the '50s, manual-transmission choices were three-speeds with column shifts and perhaps an optional overdrive. Modern floor shifters didn't start coming into vogue until the Corvette appeared in 1953. Two years later, Ford's Thunderbird also featured a floor shifter when it debuted. The first such passenger-car application came in 1959 when Chevrolet offered an optional floor shifter tied to another full-size first, a four-speed manual box. Although some witnesses claim a floor-shifted four-speed from Chevrolet first appeared in 1958, these must've been dealer-built jobs. Official listing of this option initially appeared very late in the 1959 model run. Of course, Chevrolet's Corvette had been featuring an optional four-speed, a Borg-Warner T10, since 1957.

Carb Wars

By 1957, the horsepower race had heated up considerably. Various factors helped fan the flames of this growing conflagration, not the least of which was the way engineers poured gasoline on the fire. More generous fuel flow came by way of new four-barrel carburetors, which started appearing as options in 1952. Like Buick's progressive twin-carb induction of 1941–42, the modern four-barrel ran efficiently on two barrels under normal operation, then dumped in the other duo once the throttle was mashed for hell-raising, who-cares-about-fuel-economy running. Cadillac and Buick introduced Carter four-barrels in 1952, as did Chrysler two years later for its new-and-improved 235-horsepower Firepower hemi. In 1953, Lincoln opted for a Holley four-barrel; Packard a Carter for its antiquated, yet powerful L-head straight-eight. Two years later, Packard's first modern overhead-valve V-8 used another Carter four-barrel in base form, but a Rochester unit in top performance applications.

Although a definite step forward, early four-barrels were still relatively small compared to the huge, hungry four-holers later offered in the '60s. Thus, multiple-carb setups remained the best way to really put the spurs to a performance engine in the '50s. Various setups were offered, beginning in 1953 with the first Corvette's triple-Carter design and the twin two-barrel arrangements from Hudson and Nash.

Dual fours were most popular, with Chrysler, Packard, and Cadillac in 1955 being the first to offer such a setup—as standard equipment, no less—under the hoods of their high-profile haulers, the C-300, Caribbean convertible, and Eldorado convertible, respectively. While Chrysler typically relied on twin Carters, the Caribbean's 275-horsepower 352-cubic-inch V-8 was fed by a pair of Rochester four-barrels. In 1955, the Eldorado also used two Rochesters to help bump Cadillac's 250-horsepower 331-cubic-inch V-8 up to 270 horses. Those Rochesters were then traded for two Carters the following year when Cadillac's V-8 moved up the displacement ladder to 365 cubes. The Eldorado's dual-carb 365 V-8 produced 305 horsepower at 4700 rpm.

Chevrolet's Corvette first received dual fours in 1956 for its high-winding 265-cubic-inch V-8. Chevy's passenger-line customers were also treated to optional dual Carter four-barrels that year, while DeSoto's new Adventurer came standard with another pair of Carters. In 1957, Plymouth's flashy Fury came back for its second year with dual fours as standard equipment. For Dodge's equally hot D-500 that year they were an option, as they briefly were for Ford's 312-cubic-inch Y-block V-8, in either the passenger-car or Thunderbird application.

Equally intriguing were the various triple-carb V-8s, which began appearing in 1957, courtesy of Pontiac and Oldsmobile. While Oldsmobile's legendary J-2 option was just another step ahead—albeit an impressive step—for the well-respected Rocket V-8's proud performance heritage, Pontiac's Tri Power was part of an on-going major transfomation for that division's image.

Once the makers of durable, practical cars everyone's grandpa drove, GM's Pontiac Motor Division (PMD) had begun sprucing up its act in 1955 by introducing its first overhead-valve V-8. Then, along came Semon E. "Bunkie" Knudsen in 1956. At 43, he was GM's youngest-ever general manager when he took over Pontiac's reins in June that year, and his relative youth quickly rubbed off on Pontiac's fortunes. "You can sell a young man's car to an old man," went his main motto, "but you'll never sell an old man's car to a young man." Knudsen's first move as general manager was to order Pontiac's tired, trademark "Silver Streaks" stripped off the hoods of the new 1957 Pontiacs, at the time just weeks away from production. Then in September 1956 he hired chief engineer Elliot "Pete" Estes away from Oldsmobile and plucked staff engineer John Z. DeLorean out of nose-diving Packard. From there, Pontiac performance quickly sky-rocketed.

Bringing Pete Estes into camp reportedly led to the division's rapid development of its Tri Power option in 1957. Oldsmobile had been working secretly on its J-2 triple-carb package midway through 1956, when Estes was still around at Olds as assistant chief engineer. Two months after Estes left Oldsmobile for Pontiac, PMD paperwork in December announced it would be offering a similar triple-two-barrel induction option for 1957. A mere coincidence? Only if Republicans drive Chevys.

Once it was clear to Oldsmobile's engineering crew that the cat had escaped the bag, they then rushed to get their J-2 package to market, officially making it available as an $83 option in late January 1957. Although Pontiac had spoken first, Tri Power didn't debut until March. Whatever your choice, both packages were hot. Output for a 371-cubic-inch J-2 Rocket Olds in 1957 was 277 horsepower at 4400 rpm; a Tri Power Pontiac produced 290 horses from a 347-cubic-inch V-8. In both cases, even hotter varieties of each option were listed for racing applications.

In 1958, Ford Motor Company introduced a trio of Holley two-barrel carburetors for the 430-cubic-inch V-8 used by Lincoln and Mercury—that's how Dearborn engineers squeezed 400 optional horses out of their big behemoth. Chevrolet that year also tried this trick for its newly introduced "W-head" 348 V-8, initially a truck engine revamped for passenger-car use as a performance mill only. This engine got its name from its zig-zag valve layout, which from above resembled a "W," or an "M," depending on your perspective. Either way, Chevy's tri-carb 348, with its three Rochester two-barrels, remained the Bow-Tie boys' hottest V-8 up until the famed 409 debuted early in 1961.

Beyond multiple carburetors, even more impressive power boosts came by way of forced-air induction into a carb or injection of gasoline into the air supply. The former came by way of centrifugal superchargers, the latter through fuel injection. Both of these performance enhancements were tried in limited numbers during the '50s.

Blown Away

The McCulloch Motors Corporation in Inglewood, California, was the sole supplier of the various factory-option superchargers in the '50s. McCulloch throughout the decade offered supercharger kits for a wide range of cars through its Paxton Products distributorship. And whenever one of Detroit's big automakers came looking for an easy way to boost output for its models, McCulloch was more than willing to cooperate. As the company's ads bragged, one of its belt-driven superchargers instantly added "40 percent more horsepower in one easy step!"

The first to offer a McCulloch supercharger as a factory-installed feature was Kaiser in 1954, a move that basically represented a final, somewhat feeble effort for the ailing independent to jump into the horsepower race. All Kaiser Manhattans built that

year came with a McCulloch-supercharged 226-cubic-inch Super Power Six L-head. Like its 118-horsepower Super Sonic Six counterpart used in Kaiser Specials, the blown engine featured 7.3:1 compression and a Carter two-barrel carburetor.

Forcing air into that carburetor was the centrifugal supercharger first designed by Robert McCulloch in 1951. Driven through a V-belt running off a crankshaft pulley, this unit incorporated a planetary ball-drive impeller capable of rotating as much as 4.4 times the belt speed. A throttle-activated solenoid controlled just how fast that impeller rotated, creating what Kaiser paperwork called "Power on Demand." At cruising speeds, say 60 miles per hour, the self-lubricated unit free-wheeled, producing only 1.5 pounds of boost. A little more pressure on the pedal, and impeller speed was electrically increased, upping boost to the 5-pound limit to help produce 140 maximum horsepower. Although a governor prevented impeller speeds from surpassing 22,000 rpm, company claims put the actual upper safe limit at 60,000 revolutions.

Kaiser engineers took special care during engine assembly to guarantee durable, reliable operation of the supercharged six. All components were thoroughly inspected, and the completed powerplants were extensively tested, probably more so than any other engine in the industry at the time.

Once on the street, a supercharged Kaiser could, according to *Motor Trend*, run from 0 to 60 miles per hour in 15.4 seconds with a GM-supplied Hydra-Matic automatic transmission, 15 flat with a manual/overdrive. "At cruising speeds," claimed the *Motor Trend* report, "the shift down to third gear in Hydra-Matic or overdrive, plus the stepped-up action of the blower, will take you safely out of harm's way. Skipping from 50 to 80 in just 20 seconds, the new car will leave a '53 [Kaiser] (34.1 seconds) in the dust. That isn't up there with Hamtramck hot rods like the Buick Century, but it's not bad by any rating."

It was, however, not enough to keep Kaiser running in this country. After a mere handful of nearly identical supercharged Manhattans were built in 1955, Kaiser-Willys fled the American market for Argentina.

Two years went by before forced induction was tried again by an American automaker. But this time it blew in with a vengeance. "Superchargers have come back, stronger than ever!" wrote Jerry Titus in *Car Life*'s August 1957 issue. "When these 'blowers' failed to revive the expiring Kaiser back in '54, the Detroit diagnosticians put them up on the shelf with the sassafras tea, and turned to other tonics and power prescriptions. From then until now, superchargers have been used mostly by internal specialists in private practice around the country, with varying results. But now, in 1957, the stethoscopes have been applied in the big Detroit delivery rooms, the pulses have been felt, and there's been new scribbling on the prescription pads. The tonic now being used (for extra pep) on the Studebaker Hawk, Packard Clipper, Ford and Thunderbird is the supercharger, now back in vogue." And, in Titus' words, "the pharmacist" who was "getting all the business" was once again McCulloch.

Atop Studebaker-Packard's 289-cubic-inch V-8, McCulloch's supercharger boosted output by 22 per-

It was a tough call in the '50s as to what was then the American performance car's weakest link—brakes or tires. Tire improvements during the decade included tougher cords and treads, as this 1957 ad attests. But overall handling was still average at best as sidewall structures continued to hinder hard cornering.

cent to 275 horses. These were 275 sneaky horses when included as standard equipment beneath the hoods of the two four-door Packard Clipper models offered for 1957, the Town Sedan and Country Sedan station wagon. Reportedly, these blown grocery-getters could deliver the goods from a standstill to 60 miles per hour in 9 or 10 seconds—the little old lady from Pasadena surely would've ate it up.

Packard dropped a standard supercharger from its passenger-car line in 1958, but did offer one as part of the somewhat odd "Packardbaker" version of Studebaker's sporty Hawk. Although critics may have laughed at that extended fiberglass "shark-mouth" snout, the joke was on them when a 275-horsepower Packard Hawk sped away in 1958 to the tune of 0–60 in the 8-second range. But few curbside kibitzers got the chance to witness this performance for themselves as only 588 of these blown birds were built before Packard fell by the wayside.

The highest flyer in the sporty Studebaker line-up beginning in 1956, the Golden Hawk came only with the supercharged 275-horsepower 289 in both '57 and '58. Although one of the hottest cars of its day, the blown Golden Hawk was still a Studebaker, which at the time was meaning less and less by the day to market watchers mesmerized by equally hot Chevys, Pontiacs, and Plymouths.

Ford, on the other hand, was a major player. When Dearborn officials began talking superchargers in 1957, people listened, especially so when a McCulloch blower became an option for the sexy Thunderbird's already warm 312-cubic-inch Y-block V-8. Ford's plan was to offer various hot engine packages—with superchargers or dual fours—for both the T-bird and the passenger-car line with hopes of seeing these machines dominate the Daytona Beach speed scene. That didn't quite happen as planned, however, as industry spoil-sports stepped in to shut down factory-backed racing efforts before the fast Fords could make their presences fully known. Very few "F-code" (supercharged) or "E-code" (two four-barrels) Fords and Thunderbirds were built in 1957. Dearborn's performance people basically folded up their tent after that, and didn't return until 1960. Ford Motor Company's engines may have been the biggest and most powerful during the last few years of the '50s, but its cars were every bit as heavy and ho-hum.

On the contrary, GM was more than happy to keep the performance fires burning through the latter part of the decade. While Ford was giving up on its supercharged Thunderbirds, Chevrolet and Pontiac were running right out in front in 1957 with optional fuel injection, a delivery-system idea that, like hemispherical heads, was nearly as old as the automobile itself.

Fueling the Fire

Early fuel-injection experiments date back to 1891, with the first working systems being tried by 1906. Inspiration for this work at the time came from the fledgling aircraft industry, which needed a new way to feed fuel to flying engines. Early carburetors were crude enough working on a flat plane, where they often starved out or flooded, depending on how much and in which direction the fuel supply was "sloshed" about. When attacked by the even-more-brutal centrifugal forces of flight, carburetors didn't work well at all. When turned upside down it was simply no contest. However, before fuel injection could be developed fully, carburetor manufacturers went back to their drawing boards and temporarily kept themselves in the race for aircraft-engine work contracts.

Injection systems didn't resurface until diesel truck engines started proliferating in the '20s. Diesel fuel injection was patented in 1926, and in 1930 Germany's Bosch company became the leader in the field. Various racing and small-engine applications were tested and tried in Europe immediately before and after World War II, and fuel-injected engines started appearing at the Indy 500 in 1949. The first truly successful use in the gasoline-powered regular-production world came in 1954 when Mercedes-Benz made Bosch fuel injection standard on its stunning 300SL "gull-wing" coupe.

Inspired by the classic German machine, Chevrolet chief engineer Ed Cole couldn't wait to fit America's only sports car with a fuel-injected engine of its own. GM had already tried various injection experiments in the early '50s, with Engineering's John Dolza doing the bulk of the work. Once the 300SL appeared, Dolza's efforts were accelerated, and then Cole put Zora Arkus-Duntov on the project in 1955. Supplied by GM's Rochester Division, the resulting Ramjet fuel-injection option was offered for the Corvette and Chevy passenger cars beginning in 1957. Duntov was officially made head of Corvette development soon afterward.

Ramjet injection featured a two-piece cast-aluminum manifold, with the lower, valley-cover section incorporating "tuned" ram tubes running to the intake ports, while the upper casting created an intake plenum. Air and fuel metering mechanicals attached on opposite sides of this plenum. Through precise metering, gasoline from a high-pressure fuel pump was injected continuously, through eight injectors, into the air flow just before it entered the cylinder heads. Thus, Chevrolet's Ramjet unit was of "continuous-injection" design. "Direct injection" involved mounting the injectors inside the combustion chambers. Continuous injection didn't require nearly as much as fuel delivery pressure as did direct injection.

Chevrolet's fuel-injected performance came in two forms in 1957, a 250-horsepower 283 V-8 with a hydraulic cam, and a healthy 283 horses with the solid-lifter 283. Improvements in 1958 upped top fuel-injected output to 290 horsepower. Rochester fuel injection remained the hottest Corvette option up through 1965, while Chevy passenger cars were last fitted with the fuel-injection option in 1959. Very few were built in 1958, and no more than a handful are known for 1959.

Even more rare was the Bendix Electrojector, an electronic-fuel-injection system developed by Bendix's A. H. Winkler and R. W. Sutton in the early '50s. This design used an electric fuel pump, electric timer, and electronic controls to monitor all variables—engine load, speed, air and coolant temperature, and so on—and then inject the desired amounts of fuel into the intake ports. It was first announced in an SAE paper in January 1957 after Bendix had tried a prototype installation on a '53 Buick V-8. But GM wasn't interested. Nor was Ford.

Bendix's first customer was AMC. AMC in 1957 initially listed the Electrojector as a $395 option for its surprisingly quick Rambler Rebel, then canceled the idea before any were sold. No such combination is known.

Undoubtedly jealous of Chevrolet's success with its Ramjet injection, Chrysler also turned to Bendix in 1958, offering the Electrojector as a $400 option for all the corporation's hot performers, the 300D, DeSoto Adventurer, Plymouth Fury, and Dodge D-500. Very few injected Chryslers were built in 1958, and most of these were soon refitted with a dual-carb intake after the Electrojector proved itself to be quite troublesome and extremely tough to tune. So much for electronic fuel injection. Then. The design has since become the only way to fly in the modern American car market.

Yet another fuel-injection design was tried by Pontiac in 1957. Interestingly, it was not the same type of Rochester unit used by Chevrolet but differed considerably, with the most noticeable variation coming in the ram-tube area, where Pontiac's were much longer. With its higher plenum chamber, the Pontiac fuel-injection design mounted its fuel meter down low beneath that chamber, not high up on the side like Chevrolet's. Pontiac's injection setup was also completely covered by a shroud, and its provisions for warm-up operation also differed from Chevrolet's— poor cold starting was a major problem for the early Ramjet Chevys.

And while Chevrolet's fuel injection was an option, Pontiac's was offered in 1957 as standard equipment. Standard not just for any car, but the new Bonneville convertible, yet another piece of the division's ever-growing performance puzzle that Bunkie Knudsen was then rapidly putting together. A limited-edition, high-profile hauler, the Bonneville's injected 347-cubic-inch V-8 put out 310 horses. Only 630 were built in 1957, followed by 3,096 in 1958, when fuel injection was made a rarely-ordered option before being discontinued. Bonneville coupes were also built that year; production was 9,144. In typical fashion, the once-exclusive Bonneville image was diluted even further the following year as two four-doors—sedan and wagon—joined the family. But by then, Pontiac had already established itself as builders of true excitement—and not only from a power perspective.

Chassis Development

Perhaps one of the decade's most prominent image transformations, right up with Chrysler's in 1951 and Chevrolet's in 1955, was Pontiac's in 1959, the year Knudsen's men introduced their "Wide Tracks." These totally redesigned cars featured all-new, trend-setting styling, a look that was as long, low, and wide as anything ever seen on American roads, some of which literally weren't quite wide enough to handle the big '59 Pontiacs. But Wide Track wasn't just an image, it was also a way of life, with the new Pontiac's chassis featuring a widened, more sure-footed stance. Its lowered center of gravity alone would've been enough to qualify it was one of the decade's best-handling platforms.

That, however, may have not been saying much in the '50s, as little was done, comparatively, to keep chassis engineering in step with all the extra power then being poured on. Suspension, steering, brakes, and tires, for the most part, were never quite able to keep up the pace compared to engine advancements, making safety an ever-growing concern among industry officials and governmental vultures alike.

When asked by *Motor Trend* in 1958 if he thought American cars at the time were safe, 1957 Indy 500 winner Sam Hanks replied, "Let's say that they're not safe enough." Why? Hanks didn't like most things about the chassis designs of the day, saying the shock absorbers then used weren't "any good at all," and the power steering boxes were too sensitive. "They're very quick and might cause accidents," he continued. Most importantly, according to Hanks, "the brakes on our present-day cars are very inadequate for the amount of speed the car is capable of." This latter comment then led the veteran race driver to a logical conclusion: "I don't think the manufacturers are right in putting any more horsepower in their cars than they already have. It's a cinch that we have plenty of horsepower right now."

Chassis development in the '50s, at least in the first half of the decade, mostly involved varying springing for softer rides and increasing strength and rigidity of the frame while minimizing weight. Truly major advancements, from a performance perspective, were few and far between. Antiquated kingpins began being replaced by more serviceable ball joints for the front suspension early in the decade. Chrysler introduced optional power steering in 1951, followed by GM's Saginaw unit in 1952. But while this feature made handling the steering wheels of bigger, heavier cars a breeze, especially so for the fairer sex, it took away precious road feel, as Hanks explained.

Easily the most prominent chassis upgrades involved torsion bars and air springs. The former was introduced by Packard for all four wheels in 1955, then tried again with great success by Chrysler for the front wheels, beginning in 1957. The latter equipment was part of an automatic leveling system GM rolled out in 1958, only to see it fail miserably. Ford Motor Company that year experienced similar results with its ill-fated air-spring experiment. Overall, the tale of chassis development in the early '50s was mostly a disappointing one.

As *Motor Trend*'s Dean Parker wrote in 1958, "When you consider the vast improvements made in passenger-car engines, transmissions, and body styles in the last seven or eight years, improvements made on suspensions seem pretty small—even allowing for the advent of torsion bars and air springs." The reason, in Parker's mind, involved priorities. "Between the mid-'30s and the early '50s," he continued, "the bulk of U.S. suspension engineering was aimed at improving the ride; almost nothing was done to improve roadability and handling."

The two torsion-bar designs, however, certainly had their merits. First and foremost, torsion bars don't transfer road shocks to the frame the way conventional springs do. And in Packard's case, they ran the length of the car to tie front and rear wheels together, supposedly to help "step" over bumps and jolts. Additionally, Packard's 1955 chassis featured an electric self-leveling device that automatically twisted the bars to elevate the car when loaded down.

Most who experienced Chrysler's first Torsion-Aire chassis in 1957 immediately lauded the cars it carried as being among the best handling American machines. But while those front torsion bars did do a lot to improve ride, the superb handling actually came by way of additional chassis enhancements made that year.

Spring rates were stiffer, as were shocks. Equally important, the redesigned '57 Chrysler was longer, wide, and lower, meaning its center of gravity was in turn lower and its stance more laterally sure. A higher roll center was dialed in up front, while rear-suspension geometry was vastly improved by moving the leaf-spring mounts outboard the frame. By both widening the track and relocating these springs, Chrysler engineers greatly increased roll stiffness. What they had finally learned was that even as little as a 4-inch widening of the side-to-side distance between spring perches could improve roll stiffness by 20 per-

Chrysler also tried to follow Chevrolet's lead in the induction category, introducing optional fuel injection for all its division's performance models in 1958. Supplied by Bendix, Chrysler's electronic fuel injection proved to be a total failure. The few that were installed in Chryslers, DeSotos, Dodges, and Plymouths were soon replaced by conventional carburetors. Don't be deceived by the standard-looking twin air cleaners—those aren't carburetors underneath. *Courtesy Chrysler Historical*

cent—and that without any change in spring tension.

The suspension improvements Chrysler made in 1957 signaled a trend all would soon follow. As Parker explained in 1958, "In the last five years, the slide-rule boys have started to think about handling—even learned to combine an improved ride with improved handling. Much progress has been made in suspension geometry, too. In some case front roll center had been raised well above ground level by minor changes in A-frame settings. At the rear the engineers have juggled shackle angles, spring lengths, and spring splay angles (the amount the spring points inward at front) to get precise control of rear-steering characteristics when the body rolls in a turn. We've learned to use heavier anti-roll bars in front. These gimmicks were practically untouched in 1950."

Development of Pontiac's all-new Wide Tracks for 1959 involved much of this learning and more. Of course, most of that mid-1950s education came by necessity as designers were forced to deal with the larger, heavier cars that kept coming each year, supposedly by customer request. That so much chassis development came in the last few years of the decade was fully proportional to the rapid growth, especially at GM in 1958, of most popular American cars. Then again, Detroit has never been accused of doing anything it didn't have to do.

Brakes and Tires

Motor Trend demonstrated this latter attitude in its May 1958 issue when quoting an unnamed Detroit engineer. "Our company's brakes are as good as the rest of 'em," the mystery man said, "so why should we get all excited about radical, expensive new designs?" Was it any wonder brake development lagged so far behind the other performance advancements made in the '50s?

Tires were even more of a sore spot. As *Motor Trend*'s Parker saw it in 1958, "We don't know how to make a tire that will give a very soft ride and yet will not flex and roll excessively under side forces." Nor did Detroit's tire suppliers yet have a good handle on how to keep their products together at high speeds. Various cord makeup changes helped some in the strength department, but real performance improvement wouldn't come until the radial tire arrived a decade or so later.

As for brake improvements, they happened, however trivially, and they all involved conventional drums, which always will be susceptible to fade due to internal heat build-up. Despite the already proven advantages of disc brakes, which stay cooler easier, discs would remain a European tease, save for Chrysler's rarely seen early '50s rendition and Crosley's short-lived, nearly totally overlooked experiments in 1950. Most notable among early '50s industry enhancements was the arrival in Detroit of optional power brake boosters in 1952.

If any '50s automaker was at the cutting edge concerning brakes, it was Chrysler. Entering the postwar market, the company was already using a duo-servo drum-brake design with two leading shoes, a state-of-the-art American arrangement if there was one in those days. Early in the '50s, Chrysler introduced special wheel covers that were spaced out away from the rim to allow cooling air an easier passage to those big drums. In 1956 came "center-plane" brakes, which featured an inner web for the shoes that were mounted in the center of the shoe's inside face instead of to one edge. This design meant the shoes were pressed more evenly against the drum, ensuring what the company was soon calling "Total Contact."

By mid-decade, most automakers, including Chrysler, were trying to improve their stopping power by simply incorporating more brakes—wider drums and linings, bigger shoes, and so on. This type of improvement would have to do in place of anything really important through the latter years of the decade. The only other notable changes were to lining composition and drum design. Chevrolet led the way here, introducing fade-resistant cerametallix linings and finned drums (for added cooling) as part of the racing package first offered to Corvette buyers in 1957. Ventilated backing plates and special cooling scoops and ductwork were also included.

Then, in 1958, Buick became the first volume-production American automaker to make aluminum drums standard. Using aluminum was another way to help keep brakes cool because aluminum dissipated heat better than cast iron. Used only up front, Buick's aluminum drums featured bonded-in iron liners. This design quickly helped make Buick brakes some of the industry's most trusted stoppers in the early '60s.

Okay. So as a whole American performance cars of the '50s didn't stop very well. Nor did they steer all that great with their large, nearly vertical steering wheels and big, effort-conscious ratios. And for the most part, the majority of them handled like the boats they were, rolling and weaving, or maybe jarring their occupants like trucks. This was true. We can't change that; we only go back and read about it. And what we generally read is that many drivers appreciated how these cars ran like hell—even if they did threaten to take them there directly.

2

COMPETITION PROVEN
Did Racing Improve the '50s Breed?

WHOEVER first said it probably needed to be shot, if only because the phrase has been used and abused so many times since. "Racing improves the breed." How many times have you heard this old, weary gear-head adage? But hearing is one thing—believing is another. How many times have you heard someone argue whether or not racing does indeed improve the breed?

Actually, nearly all enthusiastic discussions in this area don't really deny that a cause-effect relationship has always existed between sanctioned stock-class competition or record speed runs and Detroit's automakers. Most contention involves just what specifically is improved when a certain marque goes racing. Do "better" or safer street cars actually result from lessons learned on the track? Or is it all just hype, simply a high-profile, high-speed form of advertising? Is yet another worn-out adage, "Race on Sunday, sell on Monday," the more appropriate description for what speed tests and sanctioned competition do for Detroit? Translated, does racing improve the breed physically from a design standpoint or does it just improve sales of the breed?

Cynics have always claimed the latter. Or at least they've always claimed the latter aspect is what

Chevrolet first tasted NASCAR success in 1955; two years later, it was sponsoring the construction of a special run of *Black Widow* models. Built in Atlanta at the Southern Engineering Development Company (SEDCO), the *Black Widow* Chevys featured special chassis modifications and fuel-injected power. SEDCO shut down and the *Black Widow* disappeared from the scene after the AMA ban on factory racing was announced in June 1957.

Detroit cares most about. Among this group in the '50s was veteran race driver Marshall Teague, the man who helped put Hudson on the stock-car map early in the decade. "If you expect me to tell you stock-car racing has been responsible for most of the new features in our passenger cars, get set for a disappointment," he told *Motor Trend's* Russ Catlin in 1953. "I could state that stock-car racing has been responsible for most of the new features on our passenger cars, but I'd have a hard time furnishing proof. There isn't an official of a motor car company who would dare admit, publicly or in private, that results from stock-car racing influenced a single change. Their gain is measured only in publicity and I doubt if you will ever see the day when it will be otherwise."

Three years later, with Detroit's direct involvement in racing as heavy as it had ever been, corporate officials themselves had become more than willing to admit the obvious. As Chevrolet general sales manager W. E. Fish told *Motor Trend* in 1956, his company "currently is continuing to exploit stock-car victories as a portion of its advertising. Possibly we will find the subject a bit hackneyed; from reading the present-day newspaper ads you might suspect that we started a major trend in automotive promotion." Chevrolet hypemasters, of course, weren't the first to use competition successes or record speed runs as advertising plugs. Nor would they be the last. But by 1955, Chevy had become the most outspoken of the Detroit bunch as far as pumping its image on the track was concerned.

Of course, automakers have always been in the business of making autos to also make money. As long as they make money, we get cars. The more money they make, the more cars we get. And, yes, the cars do

Hot enough in stock trim, Chevrolet's solid-lifter fuel-injected 283 was pumped up further beneath a *Black Widow's* hood thanks in part to those special exhaust headers. Also notice the modified master cylinder (polished upright tube directly to the left of the driver's side hood hinge)—that extended "nipple" increased brake fluid capacity.

get better, too. As luck would have it, more money also means more research and development, as well as more-involved retooling efforts. While "racing improves the budget" might be closer to the truth, it is equally correct to say that "an improved budget in turn improves the breed." There. No more arguments, right?

All that aside, technical improvements do indeed trickle down through the financial realities of the auto-making business by way of the racetrack, although often these improvements are a bit slow in hitting the streets. What racing in the '50s did for tire and brake development alone was worth whatever Detroit spent promoting competition in those days, even though truly major gains in these two areas didn't really start appearing until the '60s.

Regular-production performance gains in the '50s were also in most cases directly tied to what was working best in competition as more and more hot factory options were created for street cars in order to make that equipment legal to compete in sanctioned stock-class racing. Detroit's escalating horsepower race may or may not have helped improve the breed in the '50s as far as the masses in search of everyday transportation were concerned. But it cer-

tainly made things more attractive for the performance-minded minority.

And not all Detroit watchers in the '50s were as quick to cry "greed" as Teague had been in 1953. Many felt wholeheartedly that the age-old adage in question here was completely true. As *Motor Trend* sports editor Al Kidd explained in 1956, along with the promotional value gained, there were "at least two other important features almost certain to result from" Detroit's racing relationship. Wrote Kidd, "Most important, oddly enough, is just what the current advertising claims: 'a better, safer car for you.' Auto racing does improve the breed, and the developments that Detroit has fostered primarily for racing will find their way into production; so you can have your cake (the fun of watching the races) and eat it, too (a better car as a side product).

Kidd also mentioned what many overlooked: the effects of racing on the automotive aftermarket. "The accessory tie-in is flourishing in the wake of the stock-car whirl," he continued. "Firms like Champion Spark Plug, Pure Oil, Purolater Products, Air-Lift, and others are joining in, and still more companies are getting on the bandwagon. Neatly enough, again, they'll get valuable publicity and you'll get improved, race-bred products."

The "stock-car whirl" Kidd was referring to was at the time the hottest thing going on the American racing scene, itself then as a whole experiencing a zenith. "The sport of automobile racing, once a daredevil sort of activity that attracted only a small segment of the population has quite suddenly mushroomed into astonishing proportions," read his July 1956 *Motor Trend* report. "Not since the glittering early days of the Indianapolis 500, the Vanderbilt Cup, and the Elgin Road Races has the sport enjoyed such popularity and, more important still, such widespread acceptance."

The Roots of NASCAR

The most prominent racing at that time was the eight-year-old competition circuit overseen by NASCAR. Just a few short years before, NASCAR racing had been, according to a February 1995 *Sports Car International* look back, "strictly a deep-South phenomenon: A dirt track sport for good old boys and the hooch-bearing rigs of ex- (and otherwise) bootleggers." By the mid-1950s, however, Bill France's NASCAR circuit had blossomed into a major stage for Detroit's hottest performance machines. And attendance for this show was growing every bit as fast as the cars were running on NASCAR tracks.

"Many people around Detroit honestly think that stock-car racing will develop into the top spectator sport in the country," wrote the clairvoyant Kidd in 1956. "It embodies the explosiveness of football, provides the enthusiast with ever-changing percentages and standings like baseball, and offers the speed and last-minute thrills of basketball. But just how long the stock-car bonanza will last depends, to quite an extent,

No-nonsense described the *Black Widow's* interior. Inside was a roll bar, full driver harness, tachometer, and gauges—just the things you'd want while touring a NASCAR race track.

on how long Detroit continues to cooperate." Four decades later, NASCAR racing is indeed among this country's most-watched sports.

Before NASCAR was formed in early 1948, the American Automobile Association (AAA) had been the most prominent sanctioning body of stock-car racing in this country. As expected, a rivalry between AAA and NASCAR quickly developed, then flourished into the '50s as both organizations threatened its drivers with fines or suspensions should they dare cross over the line into the other group's territory. But AAA stock-car racing was never a match for the Southern-style NASCAR circuit once it took full root. Then on August 4, 1955, AAA officials announced they would be pulling out of the race-sanctioning business, a move inspired by the horrible crash of a Mercedes-Benz 300 SLR into the crowd at Le Mans that summer. Eighty spectators died. And Mercedes-Benz itself withdrew from racing following that tragedy.

The United States Auto Club (USAC) was then formed in 1956 to pick up where the horrified AAA left off, and the stiff stock-car-circuit rivalry continued until May 1961. That was when NASCAR, USAC, and the Sports Car Club of America (SCCA) were united under one common organization, the Automobile Competition Committee of the United States (ACCUS), which then became directly affiliated with the Federation Internationale de l'Automobile (FIA) to make the world racing community one big, happy family.

NASCAR roots can be traced back to Florida's Atlantic-coast speed scene, itself created in 1902 on the sands of Ormond Beach. Known as the "Birthplace of Speed," Ormond Beach was, during this century's first three decades, the site of various world-record runs until speeds upwards of 275 miles per hour began surpassing the sands' safe limits in 1935. Late that year, the Land Speed Record universe found a new hub on the Bonneville salt beds in Utah.

Eager to fill the gap left behind once Ormond Beach became the Deathplace of Speed in late 1935, Daytona Beach city officials that winter began looking for another racing activity to bring cash-toting visitors back to the area. The result was Daytona's first beach race, a 250-mile stock-car event held under the watchful eye of AAA sanctioning officials on March 8, 1936. The race's 3.2-mile course was laid out half on Daytona's coast road, half on the beach itself. Fords dominated the 27-car field for that first race, which reportedly put the city $22,000 into the red. Finishing fifth that day in his Ford was a young local mechanic named Bill France.

It was France who helped find support for a second beach race after Daytona city fathers vowed to never be so foolish again. That support came from the local Elks Club, which explains why the next event,

From 1951 to 1954, those Fabulous Hudson Hornets dominated NASCAR competition, winning 79 races. Herb Thomas' Hornet took top NASCAR honors in 1951, Tim Flock's won in 1952, and Marshall Teague's copped the crown in 1953. *Courtesy Daytona International Speedway Archives*

held September 5, 1937, featured only 21 cars and was a mere 51 miles long. Elks Club pockets were only so deep. And the Elks' fists were tight, to say the least.

From there, the beach-racing battle slowly escalated as France started working his promotional magic. He began considering a seasonal championship circuit for stock-car racing after returning from military service in 1945. In 1946, after his plan was rejected by AAA men, France created the National Championship Stock Car Circuit, Inc., with NCSCC races held monthly at various tracks in the southeast. Two of those races, of course, were at Daytona Beach. Then, after competing in all 16 beach races held to that point, France retired from racing in June 1946 to concentrate on his NCSCC administrative duties.

Next came a meeting of nearly 40 racing men in downtown Daytona Beach in December 1947. Led by France, this meeting was held to help get a better handle on the sport, and most importantly, to come up with a consistent set of rules to govern supposedly stock stock-car racing. A new governing organization

Lincoln's first overhead-valve V-8 displaced 317 cubic inches in 1952. Compression was 7.5:1, compared to 7:1 for the L-head engine it replaced, and output was 160 horsepower. That newfound power potential, combined with that redesigned chassis, transformed Lincoln into a formidable force in the Carrera Panamericana, a grueling 2000-mile endurance run held from 1950 to 1954.

Definitely attractive on the outside, the restyled '52 Lincoln was also revamped underneath. A new X-member chassis featured bigger brakes and shocks and a modern ball-joint front suspension in place of the king pins used on earlier models.

In November 1952, a team of specially prepared '53 Lincolns travelled south to Mexico for the third running of the Carrera Panamericana, the so-called Mexican Road Race. Lincolns ended up taking the top four places in the stock class that year, with Californian Chuck Stevenson's car leading the way with a 90.96-mile-per-hour average. Stevenson's Lincoln would win again in 1953, and another Lincoln would garner top stock laurels the following year, the last for a dangerous race before it was mercifully cancelled. *Courtesy Robert Ackerson*

also resulted from that meeting as members on December 14 voted to form NASCAR, choosing that acronym over NSCRA, the National Stock Car Racing Association. NASCAR was officially incorporated on February 12, 1948, almost a week after the first of the 1948 season's 52 races was held.

NASCAR's first season was dominated by "modifieds," mostly prewar Fords with hopped-up engines. These cars obviously weren't stock, but the newer cars with factory equipment that France had originally foreseen as filling out his race fields were then hard to come by in those early postwar years. NASCAR's first strictly "showroom stock" race came at North Carolina's Charlotte Speedway on June 19, 1949. From then on, NASCAR's newly named Grand National Championship competition would feature

new (no more than a year old) stock cars only, although the tough task of defining what "stock" meant would continually plague France and his officers in those early years. "Cheating" was commonplace as the good old boys and moonshine runners who then filled out the race fields would do anything to win. The rules themselves began changing quickly and often as more and more modifications were allowed to both improve safety and keep the peace.

Stock cars from Oldsmobile were the early stars of the NASCAR circuit in 1949 and 1950. Red Byron's Olds Rocket took the NASCAR season's crown in 1949, followed by Bill Rexford's in 1950. The dominant run of those "Fabulous Hudson Hornets" began the next year as Herb Thomas' Hornet copped the Grand National title.

The Mexican Road Race Lincolns were lovingly prepped by West Coast hot rodders Bill Stroppe and Clay Smith. Here, Walt Faulkner (foreground), Johnny Mantz, and Bill Vukovich's Lincolns are being readied for the 1953 event. Power for these cars came from Lincoln's impressive "V-205" V-8, which put out—you guessed it—205 horsepower. *Courtesy Robert Ackerson*

From 1951 to 1954, Hudsons won 79 NASCAR races, with Tim Flock's Hornet finishing first in 1952, Marshall Teague's in 1953.

Lee Petty's Chrysler finally broke the spell in 1954, running consistently enough to nudge out Thomas in his Hudson even though Herb's Hornet led the way for the year with 12 wins, compared to Petty's seven. Interestingly, 1954 also marked the first time an outside company produced a special racing tire for NASCAR competition. Those tires, from the Pure Oil Company, featured a durable all-nylon cord and were priced at $37.50 apiece.

The Mercury Outboard Chrysler Team

Another dynasty appeared in 1955, this one financed by millionaire Mercury Marine president Carl Kiekhaefer of Fond du Lac, Wisconsin. Kiekhaefer put together a racing team unlike any

ever seen in this country to that point—and more impressive than many since. He hired the best drivers and mechanics and put together a fleet of enclosed transports, the latter being a first for stockcar racing. In those transports were Chrysler's big, beautiful C-300 letter-series cars. With their intimidating 300-horsepower Firepower hemi, the C-300s quickly ran away from the Grand National competition that year, scoring 27 wins. Another 22 victories followed for the 300B in 1956. Kiekhaefer's Mercury Outboard team driver Tim Flock garnered his second Grand National championship in 1955; Buck Baker brought NASCAR laurels back to Fond du Lac in 1956.

The Mercury Outboard Chrysler team then was disbanded almost overnight in December 1956 after Carl Kiekhaefer decided the public had grown tired of seeing his 300s steam-roll the competition. Some witnesses felt

The old beach/road course was the site for Daytona Beach's biggest races from the late '30s until 1959. And in 1955, few cars kicked up as much sand as Carl Kiekhaefer's Mercury Marine Outboard Chrysler 300s. Kiekhaefer's Chryslers dominated the NASCAR circuit that year, and again in 1956. Here, Tim Flock's C-300 speeds around the Daytona beach course on the way to a seasonal points championship in 1955. Buck Baker's 300B finished atop the pack the following year. *Courtesy Daytona International Speedway Archives*

he simply quit while he was still ahead; at the time, it was obvious Ford and Chevrolet were no longer going to lie back and take it from those dominating Chryslers.

Ed Cole, Smokey Yunick, and SEDCO

Chevy had first shocked the performance world with its hot, high-winding overhead-valve V-8 in 1955. That summer, Chevrolet chief engineer Ed Cole enlisted the services of Smokey Yunick and his "best damn garage in town" in Daytona Beach to work the same magic for Chevy that he had earlier done for Hudson. Yunick had first balked at the idea early in the year, then only agreed to a meeting with Cole after Bill France himself asked Smokey to help "get Chevrolet hooked on stock-car racing." Yunick then allied with Chevrolet, but not until he had Cole also hire former Hudson performance-parts manager Vince Piggins to do the same job for the GM division.

Smokey's first assignment was to get a '55 Chevrolet ready for Darlington's Southern 500 on September 5. Herb Thomas, his partner from the Hudson Hornet days, would leave his Buick (which

had just won the last race two weeks before) behind to drive the "Hot One" at Darlington. Not only did Thomas' Yunick-prepared Chevy win the Southern 500, another '55 Chevrolet finished second. Tim Flock's Kiekhaefer Chrysler was third. For the rest of the season, Chevys were consistently running up with the more powerful Chryslers. That achievement, combined with the Darlington win, was worth its weight in gold for Chevrolet's advertising crew, who then—as W. E. Fish would later tell *Motor Trend* in 1956—had the public thinking Chevy had invented stock-car racing. Cole's men were indeed hooked.

Chevrolet's racing efforts quickly escalated. In the fall of 1956, Cole—at Piggins' urging—bankrolled the Southern Engineering Development Company (SEDCO) in Atlanta, an organization responsible for overseeing all the division's competition ventures, in NASCAR and USAC. On paper, SEDCO was a division of Atlanta dealership Nalley Chevrolet—SEDCO manager Hugh Babb continually denied any ties to Warren, Michigan.

But if Chevrolet people weren't involved in racing, they didn't help support their case by releasing their Stock Car Competition Guide early in April 1957. This 22-page booklet was "prepared for Chevrolet dealers, to assist individuals who plan to participate in this challenging American sport. It is advisory only, with material obtained from some of the top professional racing experts, performance engineers and independent mechanics whose skill and dedicated effort have made Chevrolet a leader in open competition. The competition guide is not intended to encourage, but rather to inform the newcomer of techniques that promote greater safety and higher entertainment value for all who enjoy stock-car competition in the highest tradition of the sport." About the time this guide came out, Piggins put veteran racer Jim Rathmann in charge of SEDCO.

This booklet also suggested to prospective racers which Chevy model to buy—the stripped-down, lightweight 150 model for short tracks; a more aerodynamic, heavier 210 hardtop for the big speedways; or a Bel Air convertible for NASCAR's newly formed (in 1956) convertible division. It listed Chevy's hottest competition options such as cerametallix brake linings, heavy-duty axles, and fuel injection. And it even went so far as to explain how to beef up the frame and suspension within racing's rules. Who was kidding who?

According to *Motor Trend*, Chevrolet budgeted $750,000 for its racing efforts in 1957. Most of this money was spent through SEDCO, which became home to a special run of track-ready Chevys that year. Made up mostly of bare-bones utility sedans, a collection of stripped-down Chevys showed up in Atlanta, all missing

In 1956, the NASCAR racing circuit began featuring a convertible division for Detroit's sexiest droptop models. That same year, Dodge introduced its hot D500 option, which was available for any model, including convertibles. Richard Petty's father, Lee, drove one of these topless D500 Dodges in 1956. NASCAR's convertible division was dropped after 1959.

One of three specially built SR-2 Corvettes, this unique machine came about by way of GM Styling exec Bill Mitchell's personal request in the summer of 1956. Another racing SR-2 had been ordered earlier by GM Styling head Harley Earl for his son, Jerry. A third SR-2, this one a street car, was later built for GM president Harlow Curtice.

Although built in 1956, Bill Mitchell's SR-2 Corvette featured fuel injection and a four-speed manual transmission, both options not officially introduced for regular production until 1957.

unnecessary equipment such as hubcaps, spare tires, and so on. At SEDCO, these cars were then modified extensively, per NASCAR specifications. A tubular crossmember reinforcement went between the front frame horns and in back above the axle, which was a half-ton truck piece, as were the spindles. Lower A-arms in front were boxed, stiff stabilizer bars went on at both ends, a transverse track rod was added to the axle, and dual shock absorbers were bolted on at all four corners. Specially stamped (with thicker steel) six-lug wheels and gnarly cerametallix brakes were also included. Power came from Chevy's new fuel-injected 283 V-8, which was bolted to the frame using reinforced motor mounts.

All these SEDCO-built factory racers were painted in similar two-tone fashion, white on black. From this finish came the cars' nickname—"*Black Widow*."

Smokey Yunick never did agree with Piggins's plans for an "official factory team," as SEDCO was, in fact. He also would have no part of SEDCO's black-and-white magic, opting instead to keep his own Chevy racers running by his hand. Then Smokey walked away from Chevrolet completely, jumping over to Ford in 1957 for what he claimed to be four times the money Cole had paid him.

The interior of the Mitchell SR-2 is both race-car purposeful and uncharacteristically posh, what with its bright door trim, wood-rimmed sport steering wheel, and full carpeting. Notice the column-mounted tachometer.

Ford Joins the Fray

Like Chevrolet, Ford Motor Company had been making similar moves to put its face in the race, first flexing its muscles during Daytona's Speed Weeks performance trials, held since 1950 in conjunction with the annual beach race each February. An extension of sorts of the old Ormond Beach record runs, only open to less-speedy stock-class and modified-stock factory models, these trials had quickly become a popular place for Detroit's automakers to show off their latest hot hardware.

Among early big publicity deals on the beach was Dodge's feat in February 1954. With aerobatic pilot Betty Skelton at the wheel, a hemi-powered '54 Dodge Royal averaged 105.9 miles per hour for a class win in the flying mile. Skelton returned to the Speed Week trials in 1956, this time as part of a three-car Corvette team, with Zora Arkus-Duntov and veteran racer John Fitch in the other two. Duntov hit 150 miles per hour in his two-seater, a flying-mile accomplishment that finally put the Corvette at the forefront of the American performance scene.

Even so, the Corvettes were beaten in the standing-start mile runs by Chuck Daigh's '56 Ford Thunderbird, prepared by Indianapolis legend Peter DePaolo, recording an average speed of 88.779 miles per hour, compared to the best Corvette's 86.872 average. Although it was a great way to kick off the competition season, the DePaolo Engineering '56 Fords failed to make a major dent in NASCAR competition that year. Not to be left behind by Chevrolet, Ford division general manager Robert McNamara then reportedly earmarked an amazing $2.5 million for his company's 1957 racing efforts.

DePaolo Engineering put together another Thunderbird team for the Speed Weeks trials in 1957, this time with extra help coming from two sources. In the summer of 1956, Fran Hernandez had joined the firm in Long Beach, California, as engine development chief. A former partner of race-engine builder Fred Offenhauser, Hernandez had also worked as shop foreman for Edelbrock, the popular aftermarket performance-parts producer. As for the engine Ford supplied Hernandez with for the DePaolo-prepped T-birds, it was fitted with a new factory option for 1957—a McCulloch supercharger.

One of two such new, racing-inspired options from Dearborn that year, the McCulloch Motors-supplied centrifugal supercharger boosted the 312-cubic-inch Y-block V-8's output to 325 horsepower at 4800 rpm. Ford, however, chose to advertise the F-code

blown 312 at 300 horses. Adding the "NASCAR kit," made up of a hotter cam and appropriate high-rpm valvetrain gear, upped the F-code ante to 340 horsepower at 5300 rpm. The other option—identified by its "E" serial-number code—added dual four-barrel carburetors to the 312. Both the E-code and F-code options were offered for the Thunderbird and the passenger-car line, the latter hopefully leading the way to NASCAR success.

Armed with McCulloch supercharger, one of DePaolo Engineering's '57 Thunderbirds averaged 138.775 miles per hour for the flying mile in the production sports-car class at the Daytona Speed Weeks in February 1957. Another blown 'Bird was right behind, with a Corvette finishing back in fourth. While two Corvettes did top a Thunderbird in the production-class standing-start mile run, a muscled-up T-bird turned the tables in the modified-class standing-start mile, averaging 98.065 miles per hour. In the modified flying mile, that same high-flying '57 'Bird, driven by DePaolo's Danny Eames, averaged 160.356 miles per hour.

With the 1957 NASCAR season then just underway, Ford's future couldn't have looked any brighter. The tools were clearly ready, as were the mechanics. Along with Smokey Yunick and DePaolo Engineering, Dearborn also contracted John Holman in Charlotte, North Carolina, to field a NASCAR team—with fellow stock-car driver Ralph Moody becoming a partner a year later, the Holman-

King of the Daytona Beach speed scene in the '50s was local racing mechanic Smokey Yunick, proprietor of "the best damned garage in town." After helping transform Hudson's Hornets into winners from 1951 to 1954, Yunick shifted his allegiance to Chevrolet in 1955, then Ford in 1957. Soon afterward, he teamed up with Pontiac's Bunkie Knudsen. *Courtesy Daytona International Speedway Archives*

Ford's enthusiastic response to Chevrolet's escalating racing efforts involved two powerful options for both the Thunderbird and the standard passenger car line. Beneath this '57 Ford sedan's hood is a supercharged 312-cubic-inch Y-block V-8.

once the public began buying Pontiacs like crazy in the late '50s after seeing them knock the competition silly on NASCAR tracks.

Ford people had already started smelling a rat long before Chevrolet and Pontiac began dominating NASCAR racing in the early '60s. After all, it had been GM's president who came up with the whole AMA "ban" idea. Was it just a coincidence that Ford at the time was on the brink of finally surpassing Chevrolet—thanks in a major way to performance updates—for the industry sales lead after two decades of Chevy dominance? The same could be said for Ford's racing program, which surely looked in February 1957 like it was going to roll all over Chevrolet's.

After the June 1957 AMA edict, Ford's McNamara took his ball and went home, his company going so far as to postpone the 1958 introduction

of its 390-cubic-inch FE-series V-8; that potentially powerful mill didn't arrive until 1961. Meanwhile, Chevrolet's Cole and Pontiac's Knudsen continued openly playing the same game using different rules. Oldsmobile also remained a force. All three GM divisions suddenly discovered a new demand for heavy-duty parts aimed at taxi fleets, police cars, export service, or marine applications. That these special-duty parts just also happened to work well at the track was apparently a lucky break—for both the supposedly private racer and GM.

Bill France's Dream Track

NASCAR racing after the AMA ban continued flourishing almost as if nothing had happened. Then, two years later, Bill France brought his beloved home-town race into the modern era by building the track to end all tracks, the Daytona International Speedway. Constructed adjacent to Daytona's municipal airport at a cost of nearly $3 million, the 2.5-mile super-speedway was like nothing American race fans had ever seen before with its "tri-oval" layout and 31-degree banking. The tri-oval's "dog-leg kink" in its front stretch meant grandstand viewers could watch as cars either headed almost directly at them or directly away. And those high banks guaranteed equally high speeds since cornering g-forces would soar.

Bob Welborn averaged 143.198 miles per hour in his '59 Chevrolet to win the first event held at the France's dream track, the 100-mile qualifier race of February 20, 1959. Welborn's effort earned him the pole for the first Daytona 500, run on February 22. As if scripted by Hollywood, that first 500 ended in a photo finish with Lee Petty's '59 Oldsmobile and Johnny Beachamp's '59 Thunderbird crossing the finish nose-to-nose a fender length behind Joe Weatherly's '59 Chevy, then one lap down. An official finish wasn't called for another 61 hours. Beachamp was originally led into victory lane at race's end, to the dismay of Petty's people and countless witnesses who claimed Lee's Olds had won by two feet. That claim was later substantiated on film, and Petty was announced the winner of the inaugural Daytona 500—a fantasy finish for a legendary race.

Drag Racing, and Salt Flats

But legends of speed in the '50s weren't limited to NASCAR tracks. Organized drag racing competition also took off during the decade, although stock-class competition wouldn't start coming into vogue until a few years prior to 1960. Originally a Southern California phenomenon born on the area's dry lake beds, drag racing was given its first big boost in 1951 when the National Hot Rod Association (NHRA) was formed. The first NHRA national championship meet was held in Great Bend, Kansas, in 1955.

Another high-powered competition created in Southern California's dry lakes country involved groups like the Southern California Timing Association (SCTA), formed to oversee hot-rod speed-record runs. After holding its meets at the dry lakes for about 10 years, the Southern California hot-rod crowd in 1947 found themselves being crowded out by the newly organized U.S. Air Force, which had started using the expansive lake-bed region extensively as a testing ground for its newborn jets during World War II. The SCTA then simply picked up and moved its game northeast to Utah, where the Bonneville Salt Flats had been the world's home to speed since 1935.

After two year of negotiations between SCTA man Wally Parks, AAA officials, and the Bonneville Speed Association, Parks's group kicked off their first Bonneville Speed Weeks in 1949. While Bonneville was primarily the home to land-speed-record runs and all-out hot rods in the '50s, Detroit's most powerful stock models soon started showing up to kick up a little salt themselves, all in the best interests of setting as many records as possible for the benefit of the advertising guys back east. Bringing back memories of Ab Jenkins' *Mormon Meteor*, Dodge in September 1953 showed up at the salt flats with its new '54 model and proceeded to rip off 196 AAA stock-class speed records. Ford's 1957 performance blitz began at Bonneville in September 1956, when Dearborn's hottest cars established a whopping 458 national and international records.

Pikes Peak

Speed records also came in Colorado, where a mountain named after a man who never climbed it had been challenging drivers since 1916. Pikes Peak was discovered in 1806 by Zebulon Montgomery Pike, whose only other claim to fame—although Zeb would probably disagree on this one—was getting killed in the War of 1812. Six years before he pulled off that latter trick, he had tried to climb the 14,110-foot peak he had earlier stumbled across near what today is Colorado Springs. After his ascent failed, he called the mountain "unconquerable."

He was made out as a liar 14 years later by Major Stephen Harriman Long, who apparently wasn't killed in the War of 1812. After he reached the top of Pikes Peak in 1820, the only thing named after him was the length of the climb.

Like Kaiser in 1954 and 1955, Ford engineers turned to California's McCulloch company for a power boost. By simply bolting on a McCulloch belt-driven blower, Dearborn men upped the Y-block's output to 300 horses—340 with the "NASCAR kit" cam.

In 1957, Zora Duntov assembled this purpose-built Corvette racer, the SS. Beneath the magnesium body is a tubular space frame with a de Dion axle suspended by rear coilover shocks. Wheels are Halibrand knock-offs.

The first wagon trail up Pikes Peak was scratched out of the mountain's side in 1881. The first road for automobiles was completed in the fall of 1916. Immediately after the latter was finished, the mountain became the popular site for an annual AAA-sanctioned hillclimb, making Pikes Peak's Race to the Clouds this country's second-longest-running sanctioned auto competition behind the Indy 500. That Pikes Peak hillclimb runs over a 12.42-mile dirt course that soars from 9,402 feet up to the 14,110-foot summit in a succession of 156 twisting turns

Pikes Peak has long been known to racers as "Unser's Mountain," due to the famous racing family's seemingly endless hillclimb successes. Louis Unser won his first of many Pikes Peak climbs in 1934; his nephew Bobby started an even-more-impressive string of victories in 1956. Chevrolet power began dominating the Race to the Clouds soon afterward.

A stock-car class was created in 1925, but was dropped in 1934. It returned in 1956, the year USAC took over sanctioning duties from AAA. Today, the Race to the Clouds remains, in the words of the Pikes Peak Auto Hill Climb Association, "the most dangerous race course in the world, with the best safety record."

From a factory-stock perspective, the most notable Pikes Peak performance of the '50s wasn't even an officially sanctioned run. A group from

Chevrolet showed up in the fall of 1955 with a NASCAR timing team—remember, it was NASCAR's rival, USAC, that governed official climbs to the top of Pikes Peak. Chevy people didn't care, though, they were only interested in supplying even more fodder for their performance-oriented advertising mill.

On September 9, Chevy engineer Zora Duntov took the wheel of a '56 Bel Air sedan disguised with striped paint and plastic dummy headlamp and taillight treatments. At 7:17 A.M., he began his ascent, reaching the top 17 minutes and 24.05 seconds later, an amazing two minutes and 1.65 seconds faster than the existing stock-class record for the climb. But without USAC sanction, this run didn't actually "count."

Nonetheless, Chevrolet advertising gurus got what they wanted, calling Duntov's hair-raising sprint up Pikes Peak, "The greatest safety story of all." Excerpts from ad copy detailing the "record" climb included "surging power delivers safe, steady acceleration" and "with Glide-Ride front suspension and outrigger rear springs, no turn was too tough—It won't be for you either in a 1956 Chevrolet with its great safety." As for the 156 hairpin turns, Duntov's '56 Bel Air "took them all in stride, in complete safety." While Chevrolet officials didn't have themselves an official record, per se, they had proven in gravel-spewing fashion that, for 1956, the Hot One had indeed gotten hotter. And apparently it had also gotten safer.

"The Real McCoy" at Sebring

Nineteen-fifty-six was a busy year for competition Chevys, with Corvettes leading the way. It began with Duntov taking his three-car team to Daytona for the Speed Weeks trials in February. One month later, a second competition Corvette team, this one led by John Fitch, headed farther south to Sebring for the fifth annual 12-hour endurance run. Sebring's first sports-car endurance race, which was also this country's first, had come on December 31, 1950, around the runways at local Hendrick Field, a training base built in 1941. That 6-hour event was held in honor of American sports-racing pioneer Sam Collier, who had been killed on September 23 while competing at Watkins Glen, New York. Sebring's initial 12-hour race was run on March 15, 1952. A Frazer-Nash won.

Foreign cars dominated Sebring throughout the '50s—an understandable situation considering how few American sports cars were then running about. The appearance in south Florida of four blue-striped, white Corvettes in March 1956 represented the first major American effort at Sebring (Crosley had been there earlier, though with a much smaller showing), and not all were convinced that that effort was such a great idea.

"The crowds watched half curiously, half mockingly as the Chevys lumbered around the tricky circuit turning practice laps," wrote *Motor Trend*'s Al Kidd. "The same Corvettes which had looked so low and racy to them around their home towns were hulking monsters compared to the nimble competition. Just about everyone wondered what in the world the Corvettes were doing there in such fast company, and some of the Chevrolet Division officials on hand weren't quite sure themselves."

Twelve hours of racing later, two of the team cars were still standing, one in ninth place, another in fifteenth. While the Corvette didn't win outright, it did prove itself "a survivor," and that was more than enough inspiration for the folks at Campbell-Ewald, Chevrolet's ever-present advertising agency. They soon afterward began promoting the Corvette as "The Real McCoy."

Another production-based Corvette team returned to Sebring in 1957, this time joined by two specially prepared racers. One was Bill Mitchell's '56 SR-2, the other was Duntov's '57 SS.

Three SR-2 Corvettes had been built in the summer of 1956, their name coming from Chevrolet's sports-car racing program. Depending on your source, "SR" either meant "Sebring Racer," "Special Racer," or "Sports Racing." The stock-bodied Corvettes built for Daytona and Sebring earlier that year had been the first SR models, making these three the second, thus "SR-2." Two of the SR-2s were racing models, the third was a show-quality street car. All were built specially by Chevrolet for company executives. The first was requested by GM styling chief Harley Earl for his son Jerry to race; the second racer was ordered by Earl's assistant, Bill Mitchell; and the third was created as a daily driver for GM president Harlow Curtice. All three featured extended snouts and deck lid "fins" in various forms. And all three also ended up with fuel-injected V-8s backed by four-speed transmissions.

Jerry Earl's SR-2 first struggled at the track, then was lightened and modified. It eventually became a big winner in 1958 after being sold to Nickey Chevrolet driver Jim Jeffords. Mitchell's SR-2 debuted at Daytona in February 1957, copping standing-start-mile honors in its modified class with an average speed of 93.047 miles per hour. One month later, it showed up at Sebring and completed 166 laps around the 5.2-mile course at an average speed of 71.93 miles per hour, good for sixteenth place. The sleek, sultry Corvette SS wasn't anywhere near as fortunate.

Built as part of Zora Duntov's plans to put the Corvette on the international racing map, the SS was intended to match up with Europe's best sports-racers, with a real run at Le Mans being the ultimate goal. Chevrolet engineering hastily created the SS in late 1956 with hopes of first making the March deadline for Sebring. The car's foundation was a tubular space frame with a de Dion axle suspended by coil-over springs in back, an injected 283 V-8 with aluminum heads up front, and big brakes with finned drums at the corners. On top went a lightweight magnesium shell painted a beautiful blue. Duntov also managed to cobble together a much more crude white fiberglass SS test "mule," which showed some serious speed potential during practice at Sebring in 1957.

The SS, however, came standard with far too many gremlins. On race day, brakes failed, engine heat cooked driver John Fitch, an ignition coil gave out, and a suspension link in back let go. After only 23 laps, the SS Corvette's racing career was over. Then, any hopes of picking up the pieces and heading for Le Mans in June were dashed once word came down of the impending AMA factory racing ban. The SS then instantly became a museum piece. The SS mule, however, later reappeared when Bill Mitchell—by then head of GM styling—copped the car's chassis and fashioned a new body for it, resulting in the supposedly "private" Stingray racer. Like the Nickey-sponsored SR-2 in 1958, Mitchell's Stingray became an SCCA champion, with Dr. Dick Thompson doing the driving in 1960.

While both the SR-2 and Stingray were modified champions on the SCCA circuit, production-class Corvettes were no strangers to SCCA victory circles in the '50s, literally winning everything from 1957 on.

Power for Duntov's SS came from a modified 283-cubic-inch, fuel-injected V-8 with aluminum heads and tuned long-tube headers. A baffled, magnesium oil pan helped cool the cirulating lubricant. Both the car's nose and tail sections flipped up for easy access to mechanicals.

SCCA Racing

The SCCA was born in Boston on February 26, 1944. In March, the first issue of the official SCCA publication, *Sportswagen* (later renamed *Sports Car* in January 1945), attempted to define, from a Yankee perspective, just what a sports car was. This then-little-understood breed was made up of "any quality car which was built primarily for sports motoring as opposed to mere transportation. In other words, any car which rates higher than average in construction and engineering, and which preferably has open bodywork."

The first SCCA time trial was held on July 22, 1945, in Connecticut. The first official SCCA race came at Watkins Glen on October 2, 1948, and the first SCCA championship was decided in 1951. In 1952, SCCA officials signed a deal with U.S. Air Force General Curtis LeMay allowing races to be held on runways at Strategic Air Command (SAC) bases; the last of 14 such SAC-based SCCA races coming at California's March Air Force Base in November 1954. In 1955, Road America, the first of various closed racing courses dedicated solely to road racing opened in Elkhart Lake, Wisconsin. Within a few years, these venues had become home turf for America's only sports car, as Corvettes began piling up SCCA victories, beating Jaguars, Porsches, and the rest.

The Carrera Panamericana

America's best performance machines had also squared off with top European rivals early in the decade, only the site wasn't in America. First run in 1950, the Carrera Panamericana—the great Mexican Road Race—covered nearly 2,000 tortuous miles over mountains and across deserts, up the Pan-American Highway from Tuxtla Gutierrez, near the Guatemalan border, north to Juarez, across the Rio Grande from El Paso, Texas. This savage competition was open to stock, factory-equipped vehicles from around the world. From 1950 to 1954, Mexico was the place to be if you wanted to see a real test of power, speed, and endurance.

In 1950, the Mexican Road Race consisted of one class. One hundred and thirty-two entries signed up; only 52 finished, with the '50 Oldsmobile of Herschel McGriff emerging the winner with an average speed of 78.421 miles per hour. In 1952, the third Carrera Panamericana was split up into two classes, sports and stock. The following year, this division was doubled, with both categories separated into "large" and "small" categories. In 1954, the race's last year, two more classes were added, special stock and European stock. From 1952 to 1954, Lincolns literally owned the Mexican Road Race.

Lincoln had finally caught up with the luxury-car competition in 1952, introducing a restyled, redesigned model based on a new X-member frame with bigger brakes and shocks and the industry's first ball-joint front suspension. Power came from the company's first modern overhead-valve V-8. Displacing 317 cubic inches, this short-stroke engine produced 160 horsepower.

Held in November 1952, the third Carrera Panamericana represented a coming out party for the even-more-modern '53 Lincoln. Engineers improved the 317-cubic-inch V-8 considerably, resulting in the V-205 engine, named for its 205-horsepower output. More compression (8:1, compared to 1952's 7.5:1), more intake lift and bigger intake valves, an intake manifold with enlarged runners, and Lincoln's first four-barrel carburetor—a Holley model 2140—produced this power increase. In the hands of Southern California hot rodders Bill Stroppe and Clay Smith, the big, burly '53 Lincolns were then muscled-up even further for their Mexican Road Race debut.

Per Stroppe's specifications, each road-race Lincoln was treated to heavy-duty shocks and special scoops to deliver cooling air towards the brake drums. The engines were completely balanced and blue-printed, Ford-truck solid-lifter cams were installed, and manifolds were port-matched. Whether or not all this work was considered "factory stock" by the rules of the race was apparently a matter of how much race officials wanted to look the other way. By most accounts, they were more than willing to do that looking once their palms had been appropriately greased. By luck, good or bad depending on your perspective, some of this grease may well have hit the fan right after completion of the 1952 event.

Along with the Lincolns, 27 sports cars and 55 stockers left Tuxtla Gutierrez in November 1952.

Evidence of the course's treacheries came when a Mexican racer was killed on the Carrera Panamericana's second day. In all, five drivers died that year at the hands of the Mexican Mother Nature, as cruel a woman as any man has ever known. The cars themselves also suffered: Only 10 sports cars and 27 stockers survived the race.

Lincoln performance dominated, as the marque took the top four places in the stock class. Chuck Stevenson drove his Lincoln across the finish line, averaging 90.96 miles per hour, a figure that topped the previous year's winning mark of 88.09 miles per hour, set by a Ferrari. Second-place Johnny Mantz was a mere 31 seconds behind in his Lincoln. But not all were convinced of Lincoln superiority.

Three days after the race, Carl Kiekhaefer filed an official protest, claiming the first three finishers were "souped up." Kiekhaefer had sponsored the Lincoln that finished fourth, as well as the fifth-place Chrysler. He felt the Stroppe team dominance over his cars came about outside the rules.

According to Kiekhaefer, the three dealer-sponsored Lincolns had two illegal, but hard to detect modifications: a restricted heat-riser gasket and polished manifold runners. "My own engine had standard production manifolds and gaskets as received with the car," Kiekhaefer told race officials. But according to those officials, the Lincolns had all received "detailed and meticulous examination" that proved they were "within the specifications of the catalogue including the factory's commercial options." And that was that.

Lincolns remained dominant in 1953, capturing the first four spots as Chuck Stevenson won again. In all, Lincolns took seven of the top nine positions in class. Only 61 of the 177-car field survived what *The New York Times* began calling "the world's toughest race." Three drivers and four spectators were killed in 1953. By 1954, that name would change to "the world's most dangerous race."

Early 1954 Lincoln brochures described the 1953 race as a "smashing victory . . . and the 1954 Lincolns are still better!" An improved Holley four-barrel with vacuum secondaries, a vacuum-advance distributor in place of the previously used mechanical unit, and bigger 12-inch brakes represented the most prominent improvements. By 1954, Lincoln had developed a well-earned reputation—"proved conclusively in the Mexican Pan-American Race"—as the "great American road car."

At the 1954 race, Lincolns took the top two spots and another finished tenth. Fatalities also continued as two Argentines and one American were killed in warm-ups, even before the race began. But Ray Crawford managed to survive, as did his class-winning Lincoln. The same couldn't be said for the Carrera Panamericana itself. Ford Motor Company had planned to bench Lincoln in favor of Mercury for the 1955 event, but that decision became moot once the deadly race was canceled. Complaints concerning the carnage had grown too great to be ignored—at least 26 people had died in five years, most of them spectators.

NASCAR tracks were easier to get to anyway. And they weren't nearly as threatening, at least not for spectators. Life for the American breed of race fan certainly represented an improvement compared to its Mexican counterpart.

The hub of the American sports car universe in the '50s was Sebring, Florida, home since 1952 to a grueling 12-hour endurance run. Chevrolet showed up in 1956 with a production-class Corvette team, then returned the following year with more production cars, as well as Bill Mitchell's SR-2 and Duntov's ill-fated SS, shown here completing a lap in March 1957. The SS ran only 23 laps before various problems sidelined the promising racing machine.

3

THREE'S A CROWD
The American Sports Car Revival

YOU didn't need a rocket scientist to tell you which car was king of the American performance scene in the '50s. With its innovative fiberglass shell, impressive power-to-weight ratio, and intimate two-place layout, Chevrolet's Corvette fit that bill to a T, even more so after its original standard six-cylinder was traded for a truly hot V-8 in 1955. Loads of power. Serious sportiness. Plenty of pizzazz. It was all in there in spades. Hands down, this was, and still is, "America's only sports car," at least rhetorically speaking. There were, and still are, other American sporty two-seaters on the road alongside the Corvette. But not one rival then or now has ever been able to match Chevrolet's 'glass-bodied beauty as far as successful market penetration and longevity are concerned. Forget, for the moment, that this baby always has and always will be one of the sexiest things Detroit has ever put on wheels. Beneath that seductive exterior, plain and simple, is a car that stands alone as this country's longest-running performance machine. That record in itself should be enough to merit the honor of wearing the "America's only sports car" badge, even if the "only" part isn't entirely true.

What about the others?

Sporty two-seaters were nothing new to the American market when Chevrolet unveiled its Polo White prototype during GM's Motorama extravaganza

at New York's Waldorf-Astoria Hotel in January 1953. At one time, nearly a half-century before, powerful two-place sporting machines built by American automakers had been relatively prominent, although not all that plentiful due to their high prices and limited scope. Stripped down, low-slung two-seaters such as the Stutz Bearcat and Mercer Raccabout became racing legends in the years prior to World War I.

Two decades later, various fashionable "boat-tail" speedsters from the likes of Auburn, Packard, and others arrived with even more performance potential—and even higher price tags. These were cars only the lucky few could afford; for the masses struggling to survive the Depression-riddled '30s, high-powered, highly exciting cars remained nothing less than the stuff dreams were made of. From the '20s up through the '40s, practicality would push performance aside on American roads, as affordability and durability dominated.

Then along came the second War to End All Wars. Legend has it that more than one American serviceman brought the sports-car bug home with him from England after flirting with Britain's various classic renditions of the breed. The ensuing British invasion of the American market, although not much more than a minor slap at Yankee sovereignty in the early postwar years, did help revive the sports-car ideal in this country, however slowly.

Hostilities in Europe and Japan were still raging when a half dozen or so sporting Bostonians founded the SCCA on February 26, 1944. Purely an outlet for amateur sports-racers throughout most of the '50s, SCCA-sponsored competition was early on dominated by European cars as American counterparts were

In 1957, the Thunderbird's tail was lengthened and adorned with small fins, and the spare tire was moved back inside the enlarged trunk. A new bumper/grille setup was added up front. Ford sold another 21,380 two-seat 'Birds in 1957 before the four-place "Squarebird" came on the scene in 1958.

Thunderbird buyers in 1957 could have added a small gauge cluster, courtesy of McCulloch Motors, to their blown 'birds. This F-code Thunderbird's owner has mounted that cluster incorrectly beneath the dash where it won't block the speedometer. The correct location was atop the steering column.

Top Thunderbird power in 1957 came from the "F-code," supercharged, 312 V-8, which in this case is filled with the more potent solid-lifter cam. The lesser cam produced 300 horses, while this McCulloch-blown Y-block was rated at 340. Only 208 F-code T-birds were built, 14 of those being the so-called "D/F" birds built early in January 1957 with NASCAR competition in mind. All the remaining blown Thunderbirds were hatched later that summer—this particular F-'Bird, serial number 10, was built on July 15, about one month after the AMA ban forced Ford to give up its plans to race its supercharged models.

essentially nonexistent. But by 1957, the SCCA road-racing circuit had become a Corvette playground.

Early American efforts to revive the sports car in this country before the Corvette came along were meager, to say the least. No Yankee machine could even come close to competing—in popularity or otherwise—with the two top British imports, MG's TD and Jaguar's XK120, as the '50s dawned, a situation that left many Detroit watchers mystified. "There is no good reason why America should not be able to produce a good sports car," wrote *Argosy*'s Ralph Stein in 1950. "We have engineers and designers with enough on the ball to create a crackerjack car, but, from observations, it looks very much as if they don't know what it takes. With a fast-growing brand of sports-car fans, however, the demand will gradually make itself felt."

Equally optimistic for the future growth of the American sports car was famed automotive journalist Ken Purdy. He called it as he saw it in a 1949 *True* magazine feature entitled "The Two-Seater Comes Back." "Before the Kaiser War," he wrote, "when Americans were serious about their motoring, the fast, high-performance two-seater automobile was as common as the 5-cent schooner of beer, and a lot more fun. But time passed, and inevitably the U.S. automobile began to change from an instrument of sport, like a pair of skis, into a device for economical mass transportation, and the two-seater was lost in the shuffle. Comes now a cloud on the horizon bigger than a man's hand which may portend a revival on this side of the water of the sports car—an automobile built for the sole purpose of going like a bat out of hell and never mind whether the girl friend likes it or not."

Crosley Hot Shot and Super Sport

Your girlfriend just might've left you had you bought one of the earliest American sporting machines of the postwar era, the tiny Crosley Hot Shot. Introduced in 1949, the Hot Shot was the latest in a short line of low-priced, truly down-sized automobiles offered by the same man who had built his fortune selling refrigerators and radios, and who also owned the National League's Cincinnati Reds. Small-thinking Powel Crosley had been building budget-conscious, practical transportation since 1939, the year his Reds made the first of two consecutive World Series appearances. Throwing in a bit of sporty flair for his econo-machines a decade later only helped solidify his reputation as an alternative automaker.

Priced at only $850—about half as much as the beloved MG TD—the Crosley Hot Shot rolled on an 85-inch wheelbase and weighed a mere 1200 pounds. Early models featured innovative front disc brakes, one of only two such regular-production applications (Chrysler offered the other) found on American cars before the '60s. These Goodyear-Hawley "spot discs," however, proved especially susceptible to failure once dirt or water infiltrated them, inspiring Crosley to drop the experiment after 1950.

Power for the Hot Shot came from a rugged, overhead-valve four-cylinder engine rated at 26.5 horsepower. While they didn't sound like much,

Powel Crosley's Hot Shot, introduced in 1949, ran neck-and-neck along with Kurtis-Kraft's machine for the honor of being this country's first sports car of the postwar era. It was a roadster. It did have two seats. And it was spritely, even with its 26.5-horsepower four-cylinder engine. Few, however, noticed, and the Hot Shot—like the Crosley company itself—quietly disappeared after 1952. *Courtesy Robert Ackerson*

those horses were able to pull the lightweight Hot Shot around with relative abandon, especially in comparison to the slower MG TD. Road tests claimed the car could go 0–60 in 20 seconds, while quarter-mile performance was 25 seconds at 66 miles per hour. Top end was just short of 80 miles per hour.

If those results didn't trip your trigger, there was always a long list of aftermarket performance pieces for the Crosley four-cylinder, a terrifically strong, five-main-bearing powerplant that could wind up with the best of 'em in 1950. The Braje bolt-ons (full-race cam, exhaust header, and special intake setup with twin motorcycle carburetors) were the most popular, and helped cut that 0–60 time in half while boosting top end up to 100 miles per hour—a scary thought for such a small two-seater that didn't even come with doors.

These bolt-ons were added in 1950, creating the Super Sport, priced at $925. Crosley sold both versions, the door-less Hot Shot and the more civilized Super Sport, up through 1952, the last year for the

Marion, Indiana, firm. Those doors finally closed on July 3 following a couple years of decreasing demand for "America's Most Needed Car." After building 752 Hot Shots in 1949, combined production of the two little Crosley sportsters steadily dropped, to 742 in 1950, 646 in 1951, and 358 before the ax fell in 1952.

If anything, the short-lived Crosley Hot Shot had at least served as partial inspiration for Ken Purdy's aforementioned proclamation that two-seaters were indeed coming back in America. The Hot Shot was one of three sporty two-seaters featured in his 1949 *True* article, the others being Britain's Jaguar XK120 and a curious bug-eyed creation from the Kurtis-Kraft company, founded by experienced race-car builder Frank Kurtis in Glendale, California.

Kurtis-Kraft and Muntz Jet

Kurtis had begun production of his sporty two-seat convertible in 1948, its unique body made mostly of aluminum riding atop a chassis with a short, 100-inch

First offered by the Wilro Corporation of Pasadena, California, in 1950, the Skorpion kit easily transformed a Crosley chassis into a sport roadster as quickly as you could replace the stock steel body with Wilro's fiberglass shell. Estimates put Skorpion production from 1950 to 1953 at about 100.

wheelbase. Suspension, brakes, steering, and driveline where all from Ford, although engine choice could, and did, vary per customer requests. Most were flatheads, with some Cadillac V-8s or Olds Rockets thrown in. Various "hop-up" equipment was also the norm. In 1949, *Hot Rod* magazine editor Wally Parks—who would later go on to head drag racing's NHRA—took one of Kurtis' sports cars with an Edelbrock-enhanced Mercury flathead V-8 to the Bonneville speed trials,

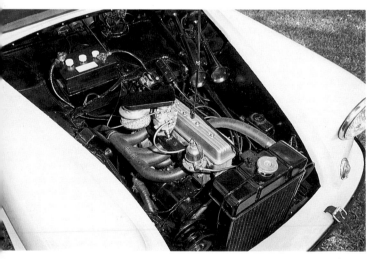

Any self-respecting kit car builder in 1950 or 1951 just could not have stopped with the Skorpion 'glass body alone, not when so much hot hardware was available for the Crosley four-cylinder. Braje racing equipment included a full-race cam, an exhaust header (shown here), and a special intake manifold with two motorcycle carburetors. Special ignition and engine dress-up was also available.

where he averaged 142.515 miles per hour over the measured mile. According to Purdy, the Ford-powered Kurtis-Kraft sportster could reach 60 miles per hour from a standstill in 11.8 seconds.

What the car couldn't do was survive into the early '50s, at least not in the form Frank Kurtis had hoped to see. His initial plans called for building at least 300 Kurtis-Kraft sports cars a year, but this prediction fell by the wayside after Earl "Madman" Muntz in 1949 made him an offer he couldn't refuse.

Muntz, once the word's largest used car dealer, had won his nickname through his various advertising antics over the radio in the Los Angeles area—"I want to give 'em away, but Mrs. Muntz won't let me. She's CRAAAAZY!" In 1945, he signed on with the newly forming Kaiser-Frazer company as a distributor. Then, two years later, he began manufacturing television sets, telling prospective customers to "Stop staring at your radios, folks!" With his fortunes on the rise, Madman Muntz bought a custom-built Buick convertible from Frank Kurtis in 1949, and it was then he became interested in the Kurtis-Kraft outfit. Once negotiations ended, Muntz found himself $200,000 lighter and one car company richer. Only 36 Kurtis-Kraft sports cars were built before Muntz took over the company.

The first thing the Madman did to the car was add about a foot of wheelbase, a back seat, and new name, Muntz Jet. Twenty-eight Muntz Jets were built in California in late 1949, most with Cadillac V-8s, many with aluminum body panels. Muntz began switching over to steel bodies not long after Jet production began as the early Kurtis cars typically were prone to dents far too easily.

Muntz then transferred production in 1950 to a plant in Evanston, Illinois. There, the steel-bodied Muntz Jet was treated to another stretch, this time to 116 inches. A removable "Carson"-style top weighing some 65 pounds went overhead, and power for most early Evanston-built Jets came from a Lincoln L-head V-8, which in stock trim put out 152 horsepower. That engine was later traded for the more modern 317-cubic-inch 160-horsepower overhead-valve Lincoln V-8 after it debuted in 1952. In place of the stock Lincoln V-8's hydraulic lifters, Muntz's men installed mechanical tappets from the Ford truck line. A GM-supplied Hydra-Matic automatic transmission was included, and a Borg-Warner manual gearbox with overdrive was available for those who preferred to do their own shifting.

Inside, the Muntz Jet received full Stewart-Warner instrumentation and what was probably Detroit's first modern console/bucket-seat layout. Equally innovative were the standard seatbelts and padded dash, safety-conscious features installed at a time when nobody else in the industry could've given

Although not a two-seater, the Muntz Jet is included here because it began life as one. The Muntz Jet was preceded by a sporty two-seat machine built by the Kurtis-Kraft company in Southern California. In 1949, former used car dealer Earl "Madman" Muntz bought out Frank Kurtis and moved production of the car to Evanston, Illinois. Along the way, he also lengthened the vehicle's wheelbase and added a backseat, among other things. The last Muntz Jet was built in 1954.

Renowned race car builder Frank Kurtis began building these aluminum-bodied two-seat sports cars in Southern California in 1949. After telling journalists he planned to build 300 cars, Kurtis then sold out his operation to Madman Muntz. Only 36 Kurtis-Kraft sportsters were built before Muntz took over.

a hoot. Its big, battleship-like frame also made the Muntz Jet as crash-resistant as they came in those days. That frame helped make the Jet a truly heavy automobile as well; at about 3800 pounds, this convertible weighed almost twice as much as many foreign sports cars. But then, unlike its Kurtis-Kraft forerunner, the Muntz Jet wasn't meant to compete with the new breed of two-seaters Purdy had talked about.

As a *Road & Track* review explained, "The Muntz Jet was not intended as a true sports car but rather as a deluxe high-speed convertible touring car in the American manner. As such, it offers the fastest acceleration and highest top speed of any American-built car available from the salesroom floor today. For those who wish to travel rapidly, carry five passengers, be protected from the weather, and who have the necessary change, this is the car." Zero-to-60 was listed at 12.3 seconds; top end was 108 miles per hour. Even more amazing was a *Popular Science* road test. With veteran racer Wilbur Shaw doing the driving, a big, heavy Muntz Jet roared from 0–60 in only 8.9 seconds.

This startling combination of performance and comfort didn't come easy on the wallet. In 1952,

Madman Muntz was asking $5250 apiece, and even then he was loosing about a grand a car. He somehow managed to bite that bullet up through 1954, building about 500 Muntz Jets along the way before finally shutting down the Evanston plant.

Nash-Healey

While Earl Muntz was busy trying to get his Jet off the ground, a much-more-prominent American automaker was attempting his hand at building an honest-to-goodness sports car. If any one car did deserve credit as this country's first modern (postwar) sports car it was the Nash-Healey, a clever combination of British chassis, Yankee drivetrain, and Italian coachwork.

The Nash-Healey was born in the middle of the Atlantic in December 1949 during a chance meeting aboard the *Queen Elizabeth* between Nash-Kelvinator's George Mason and British sports-racer Donald Healey. At the time, Healey was heading for the U.S. in search of an American engine to power a new export sports car he wanted to build. Mason, on the other hand, had the engine, Nash's 234-cubic-inch overhead-valve six-cylinder. Once the Britisher had dipped his chocolate bar of an idea into Mason's peanut butter jar full of power, the rest was history—racing history, that is.

Healey wasted little time transforming his idea into reality. Atop the Nash six went a high-compression aluminum head and twin SU carburetors, which helped boost output from 112 horsepower to 125. Underneath, he also worked his chassis magic, incorporating a trailing-link front suspension. Covering it all was a makeshift prototype shell. In June 1950, Healey's prototypes went to Le Mans, where one not only survived the grueling 24 hours but finished fourth overall, averaging 89.2 miles per hour for 2,143 miles.

Production versions debuted at the Paris auto show in October 1950, and the Nash-Healey first appeared on these shores in February 1951. Initial models used a "British-looking" aluminum body built by Panelcraft Ltd. This body was adorned with a grille, bumpers, and headlights supplied by Nash. Nash's Dual Jetfire twin-carb 125-horsepower six, backed by a three-speed box was part of the package, as was leather upholstery and an adjustable steering wheel inside. Price was $4,063, roughly twice as much as a Nash Ambassador. For whatever reason, these 1951 models also featured an accelerator pedal mounted between the clutch and the brake.

This clumsy feature was soon changed, as was the Nash-Healey's entire image, once George Mason made his presence known. Not happy at all with that British body worn by the '51 Nash-Healey, he turned again to Italy's famed Pinin Farina coachworks, the same firm that was already hard at work creating Nash's new standard-line body for 1952. Pinin Farina's results were typically stunning, and tied the Nash-Healey look to its regular-production American bloodline by way of its attractive grille, which incorporated both headlights close together within its parameters.

As for performance, the early British-bodied Nash-Healey was tested by *Popular Science*, producing a 0–60 time of 8.6 seconds, certainly nothing to sneeze at, especially in 1951. Even more performance was promised in 1952, once Nash enlarged its six-cylinder to 252 cubic inches. Behind that new Pinin Farina grille, the '52 Nash-Healey's Dual Jetfire six was rated at 140 horsepower.

George Mason had originally hoped to sell 500 of these hybrid sports cars a year, but those hopes quickly faded. After building 104 in 1951, the Pinin Farina model attracted only 150 buyers the following year. Production improved slightly to 162 cars in 1953, the year a Le Mans coupe was added to the mix. The Nash-Healey convertible was discontinued after 1953, and only 90 coupes were built for 1954. A handful of these was retitled as leftover 1955 models before the breed was finally retired.

Muntz Jet interiors were both sporty and plush, at least in early '50s terms. Both the bucket seats and center console (with radio) were firsts as far as Detroit was concerned. Equally innovative were seatbelts and the padded dash.

Kaiser-Darrin

Yet another attempt to market an American sports car had come the year before, this one also made by an independent automaker. The intriguing Kaiser-Darrin, "The Sports Car the World Has Been Awaiting," debuted in 1954, that despite initial disapproval by the main man himself, Henry J. Kaiser. As the story goes, Henry J. couldn't have cared less for the idea when he first saw the original model in Howard "Dutch" Darrin's California studio in 1952.

Kaiser's idea of a successful car involved something more like his budget-conscious Henry J, a ground-breaking model that had debuted in 1951 with

Power choices varied for the Muntz Jet. Most popular was the new 317-cubic-inch, 160 horsepower Lincoln V-8, introduced in 1952. While the stainless steel engine compartment panels are non-stock, owner-installed features, the engine dress-up and open-element air cleaner were original Muntz Jet equipment.

LEFT
Its chassis was by England's Donald Healey, its Yankee drivetrain was by Nash, and its body was by Italy's Pinin Farina. Any way you looked at it, the Nash-Healey sports car was a hybrid, to say the least. Only 506 Nash-Healey convertibles and coupes were built between 1951 and 1954. Some leftover coupe models were sold as 1955s.

practical four-cylinder power (as standard equipment) and a tidy 100-inch wheelbase. Having left Kaiser's contractual employ once before after his designs for Kaiser-Frazer's first 1947 models had been changed, Dutch Darrin had returned to the fold only to storm out again after his idea for the Henry J was rejected in favor of another. Darrin may not have approved of the resulting Henry J image, but he did see promise in that short, compact chassis, thus his experiment with a sports-car body atop the Henry J frame.

When Henry J. himself saw the results, he immediately protested, pointing out to Darrin that his company

Heart of the Nash-Healey was Nash's Dual Jetfire Le Mans six-cylinder, the same engine later offered in 1953 and 1954 as an option beneath the hoods of standard Nash models.

was not in the sports-car-building business. That might have been that had it not been for Mrs. Henry J., who reportedly convinced her husband to cast his inhibitions aside and build Darrin's little beauty.

After various prototypes were built—some with triple carburetors, a few others with superchargers—official Kaiser-Darrin production finally began in December 1953 at the company's Jackson, Michigan, plant. Darrin's body was low and rakish, with a three-position landau top and Dutch's patented doors that disappeared forward into the front fender area instead of typically swinging open. Bucket seats, a floor shifter, and wire wheel covers were included, as was a mundane Willys 161-cubic-inch F-head six-cylinder engine, a single-carb, 90-horsepower powerplant that helped demonstrate how any car is only as strong as its weakest leak.

One of Kaiser's main downfalls in the '50s was its inability to develop a modern overhead-valve engine of its own to effectively compete with the Big Three. In the specific case of the Kaiser-Darrin, its obsolete F-head engine probably would have been enough to stall the project even if the restructured Kaiser-Willys company had not fled the intimidating U.S. market in 1955 for less competitive surroundings in Argentina.

Kaiser did manage to build 435 Darrin-bodied sports cars before leaving for South America. Some

leftover models were fitted with Cadillac V-8s, a power infusion that only inspired many involved to wonder, "What if?" One of the supercharged Kaiser-Darrin prototypes had earlier reportedly run 0–60 in about 10 seconds, about four clicks faster than the stock, carbureted F-head. With about 300 horses coming from the modified Cadillac V-8, Kaiser-Darrin performance would've been downright sizzling. "What if?" indeed.

Fiberglass Bodies

The Kaiser-Darrin then quickly rolled into obscurity, but not before at least making a major fashion statement. Darrin's distinctive shell wasn't made of steel or aluminum; it used molded glass-reinforced plastic, GRP to you. First developed during the metal-shortage days of World War II, GRP was created by mixing hardening polyester resins with a reinforcing woven mat of fine glass fibers—you guessed it, fiberglass.

American automakers were already exploring the possibilities of GRP construction even before the war had ended. Henry Kaiser and Scarab builder William Stout both began experimenting with fiberglass bodies in 1944. By the early '50s, a handful of Southern California companies were marketing sporty fiberglass body kits for various production chassis, the most prominent being the Skorpion, created by body designer Ralph Roberts and Jack Wills. For about $500, the Skorpion kit could transform any yeoman-like Crosley chassis into an exciting open-air sportster.

The Skorpion made its first major public appearance at the Los Angeles Motorama in November 1951, along with another GRP-bodied creation, Bill Tritt's Brooks Boxer. Tritt first began toying with fiberglass fabrication in 1949 when he built a boat for a friend. Inspired, he next founded the Green Dolphin Boat Works in Montecito, California. By 1950, that small firm had grown into the Glasspar Company, a major producer of fiberglass boat hulls.

A deal with the giant U.S. Rubber Company followed, a division of U.S. Rubber being one of Glasspar's chemical suppliers. U.S. Rubber's Earl Ebbers foresaw Detroit's use of fiberglass in body construction and wanted Tritt to help him promote the idea. However, Detroit apparently wasn't all that interested when the two first teamed up in February 1952.

But a Willys dealer in Downey, California, was. B. R. "Woody" Woodill wanted to offer his own sports car, featuring a fiberglass body atop a special chassis mounting a Willys drivetrain. Glasspar supplied the GRP shell, and Woody did the rest, creating the Woodill Wildfire, a car that some credit as being America's first "regular-production" fiberglass sports car since it was offered complete right off a showroom floor. Most, however, were sold as kits. As Woodill later explained, only about 15 of the 300 or so Woodill Wildfires sold between 1952 and '56 were actually built in his small shop.

By early 1952, Glasspar was being besieged with inquiries and requests, a direct result of an article in the February 25 issue of *Life* magazine entitled "Plastic Bodies for Autos." Later in the year, one of those requests came from Henry Kaiser, who turned to Tritt to produce the GRP body for the Kaiser-Darrin. More important was a request from a Chevrolet engineer to see how the process worked.

By late 1952, Chevrolet research and development chief Maurice Olley was testing a standard-line Chevy convertible using a fiberglass body. In Olley's words, GRP construction resulted in "a very usable body, somewhat expensive, costing a little less than a dollar a pound, but of light weight, able to stand up to abuse, which will not rust, will not crumple in a collision, will take a paint finish, and is relatively free from drumming noise. A fiberglass panel of body quality three times as thick as steel will weigh half as much and will have approximately equal stiffness."

Olley wasn't the only one impressed by the merits of fiberglass. In the December 1952 issue of *Motor Trend*, Jim Potter couldn't say enough about the future potential for fiberglass construction. "Watch 1953," he wrote. "Plastic bodies are not only the coming thing—they have come, and they are too good not to stay."

Some credit the Woodill Wildfire as being this country's first "regular-production" fiberglass sports car since it was offered complete off a showroom floor. California Willys dealer "Woody" Woodill began building his Wildfire in 1952 using a Willys chassis and a sporty fiberglass body supplied by the Glasspar company of Southern California, the same firm that fabricated the Kaiser-Darrin's 'glass shell. Reportedly, some 300 Wildfires were sold between 1952 and 1956, nearly all as kits.

The First Corvettes

Earlier in the year, the U.S. Rubber people had brought a complete Glasspar-built fiberglass-bodied two-seater to Detroit to show GM styling officials just how well GRP construction worked. One of those in attendance that day was long-time styling head Harley Earl, who was no stranger to the two-seat theme, having over the years designed more than one sporty show car with room for only driver and passenger. But after seeing the Glasspar prototype, Earl refocused his efforts. This time, he would create a production two-seater—a true American sports car.

Transferring Earl's initial idea from the drawing board to prototype construction took no more than a year. Bob McLean did the bulk of the early styling sketches. Maurice Olley hastily brought together the chassis. Jim Premo oversaw fabrication of the GRP shell. And in January 1953, Chevrolet's first Corvette debuted on a Motorama stage in New York, impressing show-goers with its low, sporty look and innovative construction. One of those in attendance at the Waldorf-Astoria that January was Zora Arkus-Duntov, an engineer then hot for a job with GM. He finally got his wish in May 1953.

Although not directly involved with the Corvette project early on, Duntov nonetheless was primarily interested in the sports-car ideal, even though not all that many others were at the time in this country. In 1952, sports-car registrations in the U.S. amounted to only

Designed by legendary stylist Dutch Darrin, this unique-looking fiberglass-bodied two-seater was the product of Henry Kaiser's independent autoworks. Off-the-beaten-path features included a three-position landau top and doors that disappeared into the front fenders. Unfortunately, the Kaiser-Darrin sports car was limited by its 90 horsepower Willys F-head six-cylinder engine. Only 435 were built before Kaiser-Willys left the U.S. for South America in 1955.

11,199, a figure that represented no more than one-quarter of 1 percent of the total 4.16 million cars then traveling American roads. Of these, 7,449 were MG TDs—interestingly, 23,488 of the 29,664 TDs built between late 1949 and 1953 were imported to the U.S. Nonetheless, it was clear to many that perhaps the American market still wasn't quite ready for sports cars.

Duntov wasn't so sure. "Considering the statistics," he said to the SAE in 1953, "the American public does not want a sports car at all. But do the statistics give a true picture? As far as the American market is concerned, it is still an unknown quantity, since an American sports car catering to American tastes, roads, ways of living and national character has not yet been on the market." While he wasn't quite correct concerning that final statement, he was right about the "unknown quantity" aspect.

Chevrolet quickly moved to probe the unknown once the 1953 Motorama closed down. Corvette production began in June 1953 on a makeshift assembly line in Flint, Michigan. After 300 cars were built in Flint, production was moved south to St. Louis. All

300 '53 Corvettes were identical: Polo White bodies with red interiors, triple-carb 150-horsepower Blue Flame six-cylinder powerplants, and Powerglide two-speed automatics. In true sports-car fashion, there were no roll-up windows, only plexiglass side curtains to go with a somewhat crude folding top. Exterior door handles were also non-existent.

On the street, the '53 Corvette quickly impressed with its speed and handling. As *Motor Trend*'s somewhat over-enthusiastic Don MacDonald saw it, "Chevrolet has produced a bucket-seat roadster that will hold its own with Europe's best, short of actual competition and a few imports that cost three times as much."

Many others, however, were not at all happy about the standard Powerglide automatic. How could a sports car not have a clutch and a stick? This factor alone helped limit the Corvette's early appeal from a world-class sporting perspective, and the Blue Flame six didn't do a whole lot for meat-and-potatoes Americans who had already seen what a modern overhead-valve V-8 could do for a car's performance. Yankees used to comfort

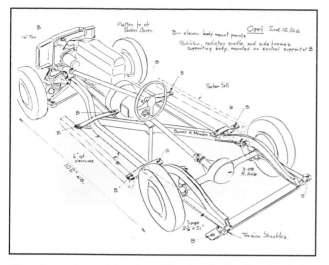

Chassis engineer Maurice Olley hurriedly sketched this layout for the Corvette in June 1952, just a week or so after Harley Earl's styling crew had presented him with a model of the car's body. Code named "Opel," this design ended up working almost unchanged in practice. *Courtesy Noland Adams*

and convenience also probably weren't too thrilled with that flimsy top, clumsy side curtains, and missing door handles.

Thus, the first Corvette was slow leaving the blocks. Early projections called for a 10,000-car production run for 1954. But with nearly a third of the 3,640 '54 Corvettes built still parked about unsold at year's end, a rethinking was apparently in order. Chevrolet then built only 700 Corvettes for 1955, but it was the last time the car's future would be in doubt.

New for 1955 was the Corvette's own modern V-8, the same engine that had transformed the passenger-line Chevrolet into the Hot One that year. A certified high-winder with its lightweight, stamped-steel, ball-stud rockers, Chevy's 265-cubic-inch V-8 offered some serious power potential—195 horses when fed by a single Carter four-barrel under a fiberglass hood. Throw in a three-speed manual transmission, introduced in very limited numbers late in 1955, and the Corvette was ready, willing, and able to challenge the sports-car crowd. While the Blue Flame Corvette traveled from 0 to 60 miles per hour in about 10 or 11 seconds, the new V-8 model could reach that speed in a scant 8.7 seconds. "Loaded for bear," was *Road & Track*'s description.

Enter the Thunderbird

While adding V-8 power was the natural thing to do in 1955 to bring the Corvette fully up to date, a little inspiration for this installation also came from an outside source. Themselves inspired by what Chevrolet had unveiled at GM's Motorama in January 1953, Ford

officials had quickly reacted with a sporty platform of their own, a sexy little two-seater with a long, long hood and a short rear deck. The legendary Thunderbird first appeared in public on February 19, 1954, at the Detroit Auto Show. As Ford general sales manager L. W. Smead told the press, "The Thunderbird is a new kind of sports car. We are convinced it will set a new trend in the automobile industry. It provides all of the comforts, conveniences and all-weather protection available in any of today's modern automobiles."

Unlike the Corvette, Ford's new Thunderbird convertible came with a steel body and a nicely fitting power soft-top or a desirable, removable hardtop at extra cost. Roll-up windows and exterior door handles were also included, as was a whole host of luxury options, such as power-assisted brakes, steering, windows, and seat. Most importantly, the classy, comfortable Thunderbird was offered only with V-8 power, this coming from Mercury's 292-cubic-inch overhead-valve V-8 with its single Holley four-barrel carburetor. A floor-shifted three-speed manual was standard, with overdrive or a Fordomatic automatic transmission available on the options list. With the manual trans only, the 292 Merc V-8 featured 8:1 compression and was rated at 193 horsepower. Another V-8, this one with 8.5:1 compression and 198 horses, was also available for Fordomatic applications.

All this totaled up to a package that was both seductively sporty and potentially posh—the term soon applied to the two-seat T-bird was "personal luxury." In the opinion of *Motor Trend*'s Don MacDonald, "Perhaps the outstanding feature of the new Ford Thunderbird is the clever wedding of sports-car functionalism with American standards of comfort."

Chief engineer Ed Cole (left) and Chevrolet general manager Thomas Keating pay homage to the new Corvette at the GM Motorama in January 1953. Various changes were made when official production was kicked off in Flint, Michigan, later that summer.

Chevrolet did little to differentiate its first Corvette from its second—this '54 model can be easily mistaken for a '53 from this angle, though there are subtle differences. After building 300 first-edition Corvettes in Flint, Michigan, Chevrolet rolled out another 3,640 from its St. Louis plant in 1954. All were powered by the Blue Flame six-cylinder.

Beefed and revamped throughout, Chevrolet's tried-and-true "Stovebolt" six put out 150 horses beneath a Corvette's hood in 1953 and 1954 thanks in part to its triple carburetors and split manifold dumping into dual exhausts. Output for the Blue Flame powerplant was upped to 155 horsepower midway through 1954.

As for performance, according to *Road & Track*, a 198-horsepower '55 T-bird needed only 9.5 seconds to reach 60 miles per hour from rest, while the end of the quarter mile arrived in a tad less than eight more ticks. According to *Road & Track*'s sporting experts, this baby was "a touring-sports car, designed to give sports-car qualities up to a point, combined with enough comfort to satisfy the most delicate of constitutions. It is an extremely practical machine for personal transport over any distance in any kind of weather."

No doubt about it, Dearborn had a winner. Initial Thunderbird production had begun in early September 1954 then ran up into the third week of the following September. Over that span, Ford built 16,155 T-birds, about three-and-a-half times as many Corvettes as Chevrolet had sold, in total, to that point.

Among Thunderbird updates in 1956 was an exposed Continental spare tire, optional "portholes" for the removable roof, and a power boost. Output for the two 292 Mercury V-8s increased to 200 and 202

horsepower, and a second Y-block V-8 was introduced. Displacing 312 cubic inches, this new powerplant injected either 215 or 225 horses into the T-bird equation, a wildly successful formula that again equated to soaring sales. Thunderbird production in 1956 reached 15,631.

In 1957, the Thunderbird's spare tire was moved back inside the trunk, which was lengthened and adorned with small, angled tailfins. Up front, a new grille/bumper arrangement also helped freshen things up.

But the real news, at least from a performance perspective, came beneath that long, forward-hinged hood. While the base 292 V-8 was itself pumped up once more, this time to 212 horsepower, the 312 was treated to some serious upgrades. With a single Holley four-barrel, it by then was producing 245 horses. And that was just the beginning.

With an eye toward the burgeoning NASCAR stock-car circuit, Ford began the 1957 model year by offering quite an array of hot performance options, for both its passenger-car line and the Thunderbird. By adding twin Holley four-barrels to the 312 Y-block, Dearborn engineers managed to coax 270 horses out of the so-called Thunderbird Special V-8. Incorporating the NASCAR-inspired "racing kit" upped that output ante to 285 horsepower. If that wasn't hot enough for you, there was more.

Like Kaiser and Studebaker-Packard, Ford also turned to McCulloch Motors for an added power boost. With its belt-driven McCulloch supercharger, the F-code 312 pumped out 300 horsepower in 1957; 340 with the all-out NASCAR racing kit. Obviously, the performance potential of Ford's blown 'Bird was sky high. Too bad Dearborn never got the chance to fully prove it. By June 1957, the AMA "ban" on factory racing involvement brought an abrupt end to such shenanigans. Ford ceased building both the F-code supercharger and E-code dual-four options after only a few hundred had escaped into the wild. While Thunderbirds did in the late '50s compete on the NASCAR circuit with the big 430-cubic-inch Lincoln V-8, the truly serious days of T-bird performance effectively ended in the summer of 1957.

The arrival of the much larger, four-place "Squarebird" in 1958 also helped see to that. Although two-seat purists may have cringed, Dearborn's decision to widen the Thunderbird's appeal was only the right thing to do as far as making a profit was concerned. After T-bird sales had reached a new high of 21,380 in 1957, production of the redesigned 1958 model soared beyond that by nearly 80 percent. From there, the Thunderbird and Corvette's paths would never cross again.

Updating the Corvette

While the early two-seat T-birds had been

Ford introduced a sporty two-seater of its own for 1955, the legendary Thunderbird. Unlike the somewhat crude Corvette, the T-bird offered ample comfort and convenience—it had roll-up windows, an optional removable top, various extra-cost power equipment, and V-8 power only. While Chevrolet was selling 700 Corvettes in 1955, Ford was working overtime to roll out 16,155 Thunderbirds.

bringing 'em running into Ford showrooms, Chevrolet's Corvette by no means had been standing still. A definitely fresh fiberglass body was unveiled for 1956, the same year roll-up windows, exterior door handles, and an optional removable hardtop was introduced. Power, too, was improved as dual four-barrels were added atop the 265 V-8, boosting output to 225 horsepower. The famed solid-lifter "Duntov cam" also debuted that year, bringing maximum race-ready horsepower to a commonly quoted 240 horsepower.

Thoroughly established as a proven American performance machine by 1956, the Corvette then blew everyone away the following year when Ramjet fuel injection and a four-speed manual transmission were introduced as options. With a hydraulic cam and the Rochester-supplied injection system, Chevrolet's newly enlarged 283-cubic-inch V-8 produced 250 horsepower; adding the mechanical Duntov cam resulted in one horsepower per cubic inch, 283 horses for those that don't quite get the picture.

What that power translated into in the real world was acceleration the likes of which Detroit had never seen before from a stock production vehicle. A *Road & Track* road test of a four-speed "fuelie" Corvette produced a 0–60 clocking of only 5.7 seconds, still a highly desirable result for most performance cars even today. Quarter-mile performance was listed at 14.3 seconds, again a hot number that would remain superior in comparison to the bulk of this country's musclecars of the '60s.

"The fuel-injection engine is an absolute jewel," claimed the *Road & Track* report, "quiet and remarkably docile when driven gently around town, yet instantly transformable into a roaring brute when pushed hard. Its best feature is its instantaneous throttle response, completely free of any stutter or stumble under any situation."

Displacing 265 cubic inches, the Corvette's first V-8 was rated at 195 horsepower. Late in the year, it could have also been mated to a three-speed manual transmission, another Corvette first.

continued on page 86

In 1953, only one color—Polo White—was offered to Corvette buyers. This changed in 1954, although the one-and-only drivetrain choice remained Chevrolet's Powerglide-backed six-cylinder. In 1955, the Corvette was fitted with its first V-8 just in time to scare the naysayers away. Exterior evidence of the new power source came in the form of a large gold "V" tacked onto the "Chevrolet" script on each fender.

T-bird updates in 1956 included an exposed "Continental" spare tire and optional "portholes" for the removable hardtop. Production that year totalled 15,631.

Chevrolet's Corvette got a new body in 1956, followed by a new engine in 1957. The enlarged 283-cubic-inch V-8 could have also been fitted with an optional four-speed manual transmission, another new feature. But the biggest news involved the arrival of fuel injection, which in top tune offered 283 hot-to-trot horses. This particular '57 fuelie Corvette is a race-ready "Airbox" model. Airbox Corvettes were fitted with a special cool-air induction system under the hood. Only 43 were built.

The Airbox ductwork appears at the bottom of the frame just inside the fender. Denser, "fresh" air was fed into that box via a duct running from the radiator core support. From there, that air flow ran through a filter inside the box to the flexible ductwork running to the Rochester injection unit. Some airbox Corvettes also featured different plug wiring (no radio was included, so neither was the typical ignition shielding, meaning the wires could run directly over the valve covers to the spark plugs) and a more convenient steering column-mounted tachometer.

Continued from page 83

Ramjet fuel injection would remain the hottest thing running out of Detroit through the '50s. Chevrolet would last offer the Rochester injection unit as a passenger-car option in 1959, while it would remain atop the Corvette's top performance small-block V-8s up through 1965. In 1958, a slight design improvement upped fuelie output to 290 horses, where it would stay up through 1960.

Additional performance enhancements for the Corvette included a heavy-duty racing suspension/brake package in 1957. In typical fashion, this group—Regular Production Option (RPO) Number 685—included stiffer springs and shocks, a beefier front stabilizer bar, and a quick-steering adapter. Not so typical were the finned brake drums, cerametallix linings, ventilated backing plates with cooling scoops, and special ductwork added to supply those scoops in back with precious cool air. Additional cool-air ducting was also offered beneath the hood for the fuel-injected 283-horsepower 283. Only 43 of these so-called Airbox Corvettes were built in 1957.

In 1958, the Corvette—like all GM lines—received a new nose featuring trendy quad headlights. Also new were the simulated hood louvers and twin chrome bands running down the deck lid. While that same bodyshell would carry over into 1959, those louvers and that deck lid chrome wouldn't—these treatments represent the easiest way to pick a '58 Corvette out from the crowd.

As the '50s wound down, the Corvette's dominance of the sporty performance scene in this country was thoroughly established, even more so after the differently defined Thunderbird rolled out of the picture. Having faced extinction in 1955, Chevrolet's fiberglass two-seater quickly gathered momentum as sales increased each succeeding year; 3,467 in 1956, 6,339 in 1957, 9,168 in 1958, and 9,670 in 1959. Crashing the 10,000 barrier—the projection Chevrolet first made in 1954—would finally come in 1960.

By then, the Corvette was indeed king; it was America's only sports car.

A restyle in 1958 gave the Corvette new quad headlights—an across-the-board trend at GM—and large simulated ducts up front. These ducts became functional when the optional racing brake package was ordered. One-year-only styling features for 1958 included the simulated louvers on the hood and the two chrome trunk bands in back.

1955
The Year All Hell Broke Loose

IT was, without a doubt, the most prolific year of the decade as far as performance development was concerned. Sure, more significant design breakthroughs had been made in previous years. And more—make that much more—power would come in the years to follow. But when you consider how so many in the industry came so far in so short a time at the same moment in the '50s, you begin to get the picture. What happened in the low-priced field alone was enough to classify 1955 as the year all hell broke loose. Additional new high-powered offerings from the bigger boys on the block for '55 only helped turn up the heat even more.

Packard Caribbean

Four marques introduced all-new overhead-valve V-8s that year: Packard, Pontiac, Chevrolet, and Plymouth. The two tag-team AMC independents, Nash and Hudson, also rolled out their first modern V-8s in 1955, although these were simply purchased from Packard. In Packard's case, power had never really been a problem before 1955, even though the fading luxury-maker had been stuck with its antiquated L-head straight-eight. In 1954, that 359-cubic-inch valve-in-block brute was producing 212 horses, only 23 horsepower behind the

Even if its imposing Imperial grille hadn't shook up the competition at a glance, Chrysler's beautiful, brutish C-300 was more than capable of intimidating any and all rivals in 1955 with its formidable fire power—as in Firepower hemi, the 331-cubic-inch V-8 that pumped out 300 horses. That output level, Detroit's highest at the time, represented the source for the luxurious letter car's name.

industry-leading Chrysler hemi. But by making the jump the following year into the thoroughly modern '50s with its equally large 352-cubic-inch overhead-valve V-8, innovative torsion-bar chassis, and definitely fresh, restyled body, once-proud Packard again became the talk of the town around Detroit.

Styling legend Richard Teague did the '55 Packard's all-new shell, which featured an updated wraparound windshield, trendy two-tone trim layout, large "cathedral" taillights, hooded headlamps, and a gleaming, modern grille that used a sporty "egg-crate" layout on some models. While Teague's final product was upstaged by various other styling updates that year, all critics agreed it represented a marked improvement over what had come before from Packard.

Contracted engineer William Allison designed the Torsion-Level Ride chassis, which used two 9-foot-long torsion bars to tie the suspension's front and rear control arms together, allowing both ends of the car to work in unison over bumps and jolts. When a front tire hit a bump, it transferred its motion not directly to the frame, as typical springs do, but to its trailing wheel on that side through the torsion bar, which then helped keep the rear tire from over-reacting to that same rolling input. The torsion bars were also controlled by an electric self-leveling motor that twisted them "tighter" to supply more spring tension once the car was loaded down. While Packard's Torsion-Level design was intended to supply a luxury ride, performance potential was in there, too.

According to *Motor Life* road testers, the "ride calls for a flat and unequivocal statement: it is the best among current American cars." But they also pointed out that "handling qualities are definitely superior and

89

Although it weighed in at more than two tons, Chrysler's first 300 was a force to be reckoned with. Performance was only a few ticks behind the much lighter Corvette. Total C-300 production was 1725. Beginning in 1956, the letter-series designation was changed to 300B, with each succeeding model year advancing another notch up the alphabet. The last 300, the 300L, was built in 1965. There was no 300I to avoid confusion with the Roman numeral "I."

As the name implied, the C-300 featured 300 horses beneath its hood, courtesy of Chrysler's 331 cubic inch Firepower hemi V-8. Hiding underneath that large air cleaner (which is incorrect—an oil-bath unit was actually used) are two Carter four-barrel carburetors.

Leather seating, a padded dash, and a 150-mile-per-hour speedometer were standard 300 features in 1955. Notice the automatic shift lever protruding from the instrument panel just to the left of the radio. All early 300s were automatic-equipped.

the car is obviously easier to control, as the torsion bars wind and unwind. Body heel is so slight that a new feeling of flat cornering is present."

As for Packard's overhead-valve V-8, it was some nine years in the making, and was specifically designed with future displacement growth in mind. In 1955, it was offered in two sizes, with a smaller 320-cubic-inch version available for the lesser Clipper lines, the big-dog 352 for the top models. Engineers claimed there were at least 400 cubic inches possible, maybe more, from this engine, which was as durable as it was powerful. Packard demonstrated these merits in an October 1954 test sanctioned by the **AAA.** In this typically well publicized test, a '55 Packard covered 25,000 miles in 238 hours, 41 minutes, and 44.3 seconds, averaging 104.737 miles per hour for the trip. All told, this endurance run established 147 national and worldwide performance records.

Power was clearly plentiful. With a single Carter four-barrel carburetor and 8.5:1 compression, the Clipper Custom's 352-cubic-inch V-8 was rated at 245 horsepower. The Packard line's 352 used a Rochester four-barrel to produce 260 horses. And that wasn't all. With two Rochester four-barrels, the 352 V-8 put out 275 horsepower, second only to Chrysler's 300-horsepower Firepower hemi in 1955. Putting those 275 horses to good use as standard equipment was Packard's high-profile, limited-edition convertible, the Caribbean, a sporty creation that had first appeared in 1953.

Introduced in January that year, with deliveries beginning in March, the first Caribbean was a regular-production response to the Pan American show car designed in 1952 by Richard Arbib of Henney Motor Company, Packard's commercial body supplier. Arbib created the Pan American by lowering, sectioning, and dechroming a stock Packard 250 convertible. After this

sleek, sexy machine wowed everyone on the auto-show circuit in 1952, Packard head James Nance decided to offer a similar model in limited-edition form.

Newly hired chief stylist Dick Teague rose to the challenge, knowing he'd never be able to perform the costly modifications Arbib did, considering typical budgetary restraints. Although Teague couldn't lower the suspension or section the body, he could use Arbib's hood scoop, wire wheels, Continental spare tire, and dechromed appearance. Beginning with a '53 Mayfair convertible, he did at least add some additional exclusive flair by opening up the rear wheel houses to match the semi-circle front fender design. All four wheel arches were then adorned with large chrome trim.

All early Caribbeans were produced by the Mitchell-Bentley company in Ionia, Michigan. Into the Ionia works went unfinished '53 Packard convertible bodies, out came completed Caribbeans, priced at $5210, $1724 more than a typical Packard drop-top in 1953. For that price, a status-hungry customer also got a 180-horsepower 327-cubic-inch straight-eight with 8:1 compression and a Carter four-barrel carburetor, just enough of an engine to keep the heavy Caribbean from falling too far behind a Cadillac or Chrysler counterpart. A three-speed manual transmission with overdrive was standard, and the Ultramatic automatic was optional. In all, Mitchell-Bentley built 750 Caribbeans in 1953.

Another 400 Caribbeans left Ionia in 1954, this time with a body suited for two-toning (most were) on the outside and Packard's enlarged, 359-cubic-inch L-head eight with its 212 horses beneath that scooped hood. Ultramatic was the only transmission available for the second-edition Caribbean.

Nance once more limited the production run in 1955, only to soon regret that choice. Although by then no longer a custom-built product of Mitchell-Bentley, the production-based, third-edition Caribbean nonetheless

At the opposite end of the price spectrum from Chrysler's 300 was Chevrolet's all-new '55 model with its equally new over-head-valve V-8. Fresh, exciting, "Motoramic" styling. Radically improved mechanicals. Competitive V-8 power. All this and more in the low-priced ranks? Once the "Hot One" arrived, things would never again be the same in Detroit.

Long a sales leader based on its affordable reliability, Chevrolet's mundane image disappeared overnight once the division's first modern overhead-valve V-8 appeared. Chevy's high-winding 265-cubic-inch V-8 produced 162 horses in standard tune and 180 horsepower with the optional "Power Pack" (a four-barrel carburetor and dual exhausts).

featured all of Packard's best—fresh styling atop that torsion-bar chassis fitted with the 275-horsepower 352 V-8. Behind that twin-carb powerplant was the equally new Twin-Ultramatic automatic transmission, the work of a young engineer named John DeLorean. On top was triple-tone paint, dual aerials and exhausts, twin hood scoops, and Teague's egg-crate grille. All power options were standard, while wire wheels were optional, as was air conditioning. Totaled up, the '55 Caribbean package was indeed a desirable one, so much so that the limited run quickly sold out in only four months.

Packard carted out the Caribbean convertible one more time in 1956, and complemented it for the first time with a hardtop running mate. Production was 276 convertibles and 263 hardtops. To their last days, the Caribbeans were eye-catching, high-priced boulevard cruisers costing just short of $6000. Even if Packard had built more in 1955 and 1956, not too many Americans could've found the cash for that kind of performance 40 years ago.

Turning Chevrolet Around

More important from the perspective of the average car buyer in need of a little speed in 1955 was the overnight sensation created in the low-priced ranks by Chevrolet. As the most affordable rung on GM's divisional ladder, Chevy's role had long been simply to put as many reliable, practical cars into public hands as possible. That it did; as 1954 was winding down, company ads proclaimed proudly that, "for the 19th straight year, more people bought Chevrolets than any other car!" The year before, the division had rolled its 29 millionth car off the line on June 9. The 30 millionth would follow by year's end. If it ain't broke, don't fix it, right?

Yes and no. While Chevrolet continued leading the industry sales race into the mid-'50s, fellow low-priced rival Ford was rapidly gaining ground by 1953. And by some accounts, Dearborn's affordable line did actually unseat Chevrolet atop industry rankings in 1954—only a little number shuffling and fast talking allowed Chevy's propaganda masters to run that "19th straight year" ad with little regard as to whether or not it was actually true. As it was, the division sold nearly 1.5 million cars in 1954; with that kind of volume, who could've cared about who beat who on paper?

GM's brain trust, that was who. As early as December 1951 they had begun planning to "turn Chevrolet around," first from an engineering standpoint. In April 1952, Ed Cole was moved over from Cadillac to become Chevrolet's chief engineer. He was joined soon afterward by another Cadillac engineer, Harry Barr. It was no coincidence that both Cole and Barr had played major roles in Cadillac's development of its short-stroke, overhead-valve V-8, which had debuted in 1949. Head of Chevrolet styling was Clare MacKichan. With the right people then in the right places, GM next reportedly earmarked $300 million to totally redesign the Chevrolet for 1955.

Any way you looked at it—on top, underneath, inside, beneath the hood—the so-called Motoramic Chevrolet was as new as they came, especially so considering the yeoman-like, old-reliable models it replaced. Barr's redesigned chassis was a great place to start. Although the 1955 frame weighed 18 percent less than its 1954 forerunner it was 50 percent more rigid. And gone were the antiquated torque-tube drive and kingpins used in 1954; in their place were modern ball-joints and Hotchkiss drive. Front-suspension geometry was also reworked considerably for excellent anti-dive characteristics, while the lengthened leaf springs in back were relocated outside the frame rails in "outrigger" fashion to increase roll stiffness.

As improved as its chassis was, the '55 Chevy—soon labeled the Hot One—was quicker to attract eager buyers with its equally new body, a trendy creation featuring many of GM styling mogul Harley Earl's pet cues. Among these was the car's low, sweeping roofline; equally low beltline with that trademark "notch" directly ahead of each rear quarter; and the Sweep-Sight wraparound windshield. Earl was also credited with adding the Ferrari-inspired egg-crate grille, a design then slightly ahead of its time. While most today feel that grille looks every bit as hot as the car itself, many critics in 1955 didn't like it at all, leading MacKichan's men to try again in 1956 with a different layout featuring a little less crate and a bit more chrome.

The real attraction, however, came in the engine compartment where optional power was supplied by Chevrolet's first modern overhead-valve V-8, the real inspiration for the Hot One reputation. Displacing 265 cubic inches, this lightweight, compact powerplant could wind out like no other V-8 then around. Its very short stroke—only 3 inches—helped make that high rev limit possible, as did its innovative valve-train layout.

Instead of using typical rocker arms mounted on a central rocker shaft, Chevrolet's 265 V-8 featured individual stamped-steel rockers, each mounted separately on a ball-pivot stud. This not only meant that deflection wouldn't be passed on from one rocker to others via that shaft, it also translated into a tidy weight loss—fewer parts mean less weight. Along with being lighter, the ball-stud rocker layout was obviously less complicated than shaft-mounted designs—both these aspects contributed to easy revving.

Although commonly credited to Chevrolet today, the ball-stud rocker idea first used in 1955 actually came from Pontiac Motor Division, which had been working on its own overhead-valve V-8 since 1946. Pontiac's V-8 design work was headed by Mark Frank, with Ed Windeler, George Roberts, Malcolm "Mac" McKellar, and Clayton Leach making major contributions. It was Leach who had invented the ball-stud rocker-arm design in 1948. Leach's idea was then applied to the design project intended to bring Pontiac into the modern market. By early 1951, the division appeared ready to have its first overhead-valve V-8 up and running for 1953, but developmental problems and budget factors ended up delaying that debut by two years. And then, as work on Pontiac's ensuing 287-cubic-inch overhead-valve V-8 neared completion, Ed Cole's men picked up on Pontiac's rocker design for their own project.

Attractive in its own right, Pontiac's new V-8 for 1955 was just one step in a multi-year ride up from the hum-drums to a respected performance reputation. The ball really got rolling once Bunkie Knudsen arrived in late 1956 to lead the division. In Pontiac's case, 1957 would be its first really big performance year.

Chevrolet, however, wouldn't wait that long, its high-winding 265 V-8 in 1955 chomping at the bit to prove just how hot things could get for the competition. In base form, with 8:1 compression and a two-barrel carburetor, the 265 produced 162 horsepower at 4400 rpm. But if more was the goal, more was available by way of a Power Pack option that added a four-barrel carburetor and dual exhausts. Maximum output with this equipment in place was 180 horses at 4600 rpm. Throw in the optional overdrive for the three-speed manual and 4.11:1 gears in back and there was no stopping you. And to think all this performance cost only $2300 in 1955.

A triple-digit top-end had never come this cheap. Nor had cutting-edge passenger-car acceleration, excellent handling, and dashing good looks. In the ever-present opinion of *Mechanix Illustrated*'s Tom

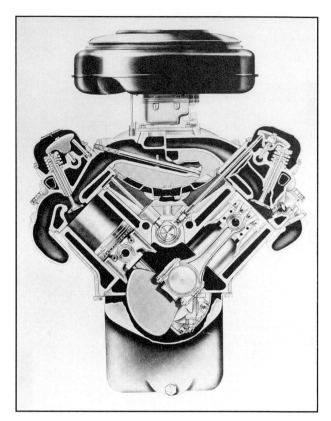

The stamped-steel individual ball-stud rocker arms that helped Chevy's 265 V-8 wind out like few others actually came from Pontiac engineers. The design was created for PMD's first modern overhead-valve V-8, itself introduced for 1955. Once Ed Cole's men discovered what Pontiac was doing, they simply had to have those ball-stud rockers for themselves. Thus, Chevrolet still commonly receives credit for the idea.

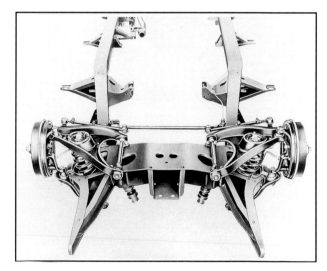

Along with its hot, high-winding V-8, the Motoramic Chevrolet in 1955 also was fitted with a redesigned chassis featuring state-of-the-art coil-spring SLA (short arm/long arm) suspension up front and "outrigger" leaf springs (mounted outboard the frame rails) in back. The frame itself was new and much more rigid than before.

McCahill, the Hot One was "the most glamorous look-ing and hottest performing Chevy to come down the pike." *Popular Mechanics*'s Floyd Clymer called it the "best-handling Chevrolet I have ever driven." *Motor Trend* went even further, proclaiming the '55 Chevrolet (along with the '55 Mercury) to be Detroit's best road car, period. Even more well-earned publicity came when Chevrolet's all-new model was chosen as the prestigious pace car for the 1955 Indianapolis 500.

On the street, the hottest '55 Chevy was virtually unbeatable. As *Road & Track* explained, "It certainly appears that a Chevrolet V-8 with [the] optional 180-horsepower engine and 4.11 axle will out-accelerate any American car on the market today!" *Road & Track*'s road test results were startling, to say the least: 0–60 in 9.7 seconds, 17.2 ticks for the quarter mile. Any American car running under 10 seconds from rest to 60 miles per hour was news enough in those days. That this American car was a Chevrolet—just one year away from its mundane "Stovebolt" days—was certainly grounds to write home to mother.

Those with about $1500 more to spend in 1955 would've been equally impressed by Chevrolet's Corvette, which was brought back to life thanks to the arrival of the division's hot, new 265-cubic-inch powerplant. Putting 195 V-8 horses beneath a fiber-glass hood that year was just what the doctor ordered for the sputtering fiberglass sports car, even more so considering that Ford's all-new two-seater was then about to steal what little was left of Chevy's sporty thunder. Thunderbirds from the beginning came with V-8 power or no power at all, while the Corvette had turned off many in 1954 with its six-cylinder engine and Powerglide automatic transmission. From 1955 on, however, the Corvette was off and running with a standard V-8 of its own. And America's only sports car would never be head-ed again.

Plymouth's "Forward Look" Styling

A similar revival also occurred in Detroit's low-priced ranks in 1955. And once more it came in part through the introduction of yet another all-new over-head-valve V-8. Chrysler's most affordable division, Plymouth, had been running just about as low as it goes in 1954, with sales dipping by almost half of 1953's levels. From 1946 to 1953, Plymouth had been maintaining a strong third in industry sales rankings behind Chevy and Ford. With the drop in 1954, it fell to fifth as Buick and Olds leapfrogged ahead, they with their trend-setting styling, wraparound wind-shields, V-8 power, and automatic transmissions. Something clearly had to be done to stem the tide. Luckily Chrysler president "Tex" Colbert and styling chief Virgil Exner had both already been looking for-ward into the future.

Chevrolet wasn't alone in the low-priced field as far as total transformations were concerned in 1955. Plymouth, too, received all-new styling and its first modern over-head-valve V-8. Many felt the all-new '55 Plymouth was every bit as attractive inside and out as its all-new coun-terpart from Chevrolet.

It was Plymouth's new "Forward Look" styling, penned by Maury Baldwin and Bud Gitschlag under the guiding eye of Exner, that helped turn things around in 1955. Longer, lower, and wider, with a rak-ish flair typical of all Exner's Chryslers, the all-new '55 Plymouth was every bit as striking as its all-new rival from Chevrolet. Just one look was all the Society of Illustrators needed to proclaim the '55 Plymouth as being "The Most Beautiful Car of the Year," an honor that represented the first time this group had extended an award to the automotive field in its 53-year history.

Beauty beneath the skin ran deep. Revised chassis features included big, optional 11-inch front drums

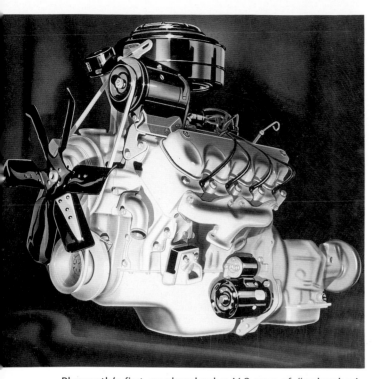

Plymouth's first overhead-valve V-8 was of "polyspherical-head" design, as opposed to the hemispherical heads used by Chrysler's other divisions. This layout meant only one rocker shaft was required for these canted valves (hemi V-8s used twin rocker shafts). And it also meant that spark plugs could be angled out to the side below the valve covers. The centrally located park plugs in hemi V-8s were buried deep within the valve covers.

and outboard-mounted 2-inch-wide leaf springs that lowered the car's center of gravity. Additional new options included air conditioning, dual exhausts, power windows, and power seats. And for $165, a Plymouth buyer could've added the two-speed Powerflite automatic transmission, a major improvement over the antiquated Hy-Drive semi-automatic offered in previous years.

As expected, the biggest news came beneath the hood. There, Plymouth offered three different overhead-valve V-8s, the first a 241-cubic-inch version with 157 horsepower, which was early in the year replaced by a larger, 260-cubic-inch rendition rated at 167 horses. Adding the optional Power Pak (a Carter four-barrel carburetor and dual exhausts), boosted the 260's output to 177 horsepower.

All three of these V-8s differed from those used by Chrysler, Dodge, and DeSoto in that they featured polyspherical (instead of hemispherical) combustion chambers. Accordingly, Plymouth's new V-8 took on the "poly-head" nickname. Although the valves in a polyhead V-8 were canted in similar fashion to its hemi

Dodges were no slouches after they first received hemi V-8 power in 1953. In 1955, Dodge's top Red Ram hemi V-8 produced 193 horsepower. According to *Motor Trend*, this was enough power to propel an automatic-equipped '55 Custom Royal through the quarter-mile in 16.2 seconds. Top end was listed at 101.8 miles per hour.

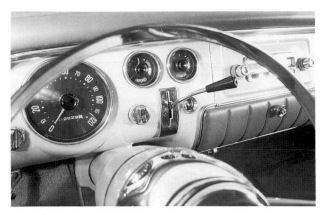

Beginning in 1955, Chrysler Corporation cars featured various slightly odd automatic transmission controls. That year it was this dash-mounted lever. The following year, the lever was traded for dash-mounted pushbuttons.

cousins, the angle wasn't nearly as severe, meaning twin rocker shafts weren't required atop each cylinder head. This in turn meant there was more room to angle the spark plugs out away from the combustion chambers through the cylinder head's exterior wall in more conventional fashion. Poly-head plugs were accessible just below the valve covers' lower edges; hemi plugs were literally buried deep within the valve covers.

Demonstrating what a modern V-8 could do for popularity in 1955, 61 percent of the Plymouths sold that year were equipped with a poly-head powerplant. Total production, by the way, jumped by 52 percent to more than 700,000, good enough for a rise back to fourth. A return to third would come two years later.

Chrysler 300

An even more serious shot in the arm for Chrysler performance in 1955 came all the way at the top, some $2000 above the V-8 Plymouth. A beast of a beauty, the first of Chrysler's high-priced, high-powered 300 letter-series cars was introduced to the public on January 17, 1955, as an impressive display of just what can happen when the best of both worlds—performance and luxury—meet.

Virgil Exner had already spent a hundred million or so Chrysler dollars restyling the corporation's 1955 models when chief engineer Robert MacGregor Rodger came up with the idea of marrying serious speed and posh prestige. Rodger was no stranger to performance, having been heavily involved in the design and development of Chrysler's Firepower hemi. In his opinion, putting Chrysler atop the '50s performance heap was simply a matter of incorporating the corporation's existing hot hardware into a high-profile automobile capable of turning heads with its looks and its acceleration.

Exner liked Rodger's idea, as did Chrysler division manager Ed Quinn. But Exner's "100-Million-Dollar Look" had already done a number on Chrysler's retooling budget. Quinn, nonetheless, gave Rodger's project a go-ahead with the stipulation that creative costs be kept low. The buck was then passed to Cliff Voss, head of the Chrysler Imperial design studio, who, along with Rodger and production chief Tom Poirier, managed to pull off the feat in classic fashion.

Combining some lavish Imperial features with a hot 331-cubic-inch hemi V-8, Chrysler's first luxo hot rod was named for its industry-leading output rating, 300 horsepower. Officially, the car was labeled the "C-300," undoubtedly in honor of Briggs Cunningham's various hemi-powered racers of the early '50s, all of which were identified by an appropriate "C" prefix. (Concerning the C-300, *Auto Age*'s July 1955 issue asked, "Is it the 1955 Cunningham?") When the second-edition 300 appeared for 1956, the name was "300B," beginning a progression that followed in alphabetical order for each year to follow. With the exception of omitting the letter "I," supposedly to avoid confusion with the Roman numeral "I," Chrysler's letter car legacy continued through 11 model runs, ending in 1965 with the 300L.

Even though Rodger and Voss saved considerable cash by using existing pieces, the C-300 came off looking—and running—like a million bucks. Based on a New Yorker bodyshell, the C-300 mounted an attractive egg-crate Imperial grille and understated Windsor body-side trim. Inside was a padded dashboard, a 150-mile-per-hour speedometer, and tan leather appointments. Heavy-duty underpinnings, including Imperial front suspension, were also standard. And all 1,692 U.S.-sold C-300s (exports totaled 33) came with two-speed Powerflite automatic transmissions, bringing the base price to a hefty $4,055. Only three colors were offered; Tango Red, Platinum White, and black.

Extra-cost baubles aimed at the luxury-minded crowd included a radio, heater, and power steering, a handy package priced at $294. A few additional dollars would've also added a power seat, brakes, and windows, and glittering Imperial wire wheels—which, incidentally, helped cool the big drum brakes.

Rodger's contribution was the 300-horsepower 331 hemi with its twin Carter four-barrel carbs, high-lift cam with solid lifters, 8.5:1 compression, and dual low-restriction exhausts. Standard rear-axle ratio was 3.36:1, with four optional gearsets as low as 4.1:1 available. In Chrysler's words, the sum of these parts equaled "America's greatest performing motor car . . . with the speed of the wind, the maneuverability of a polo pony, the power to pass on the road safely, an all-around performance quite unlike anything you will find available here in America or abroad."

Built as "a sports touring car designed to bring Chrysler the benefit of a high-performance reputa-

Studebaker's creative fellows took their shot at the sporty market in 1955, introducing the tri-toned President Speedster, a heavily chromed variant of the same quasi-classic coupe first styled by Raymond Loewy Studio's Robert Bourke in 1953. The simulated wire wheelcovers were part of the package, as were the foglamps up front and the additional chrome around the roof's trailing edge.

tion," the C-300 did not disappoint. Even at 4300 pounds, it was capable of nearly matching the much lighter V-8 Corvette in all-out performance. Able to run 0–60 in 9 seconds, Chevrolet's fiberglass two-seater could complete the quarter mile in 17.2 seconds at 81.5 miles per hour. Not far behind, the palatial C-300 with room for the entire family turned the quarter in 17.6 seconds at 82 miles per hour and went from rest to 60 miles per hour in 9.6 seconds.

Unusually excited beyond description, Tom McCahill called the big 300 "the most powerful sedan in the world, and the fastest, teamed up with rock-crushing suspension and a competition engine capable of yanking Bob Fulton's steamboat over the George Washington Bridge." With that established, the *Mechanix Illustrated* scribe then continued, explaining that "this is definitely not the car for Henrietta Blushbottom, your maiden schoolmarm aunt, to use for hustling up popsicles. In fact, the 300 is not a car

for the typical puddling male to use. This is a hard-boiled, magnificent piece of semi-competition transportation, built for the real automotive connoisseur."

Semi-competition? Chrysler's first 300 went right to the track with ease, first setting a flying-mile speed record of 127.58 miles per hour on the beach at Daytona. Next came complete domination of NASCAR and AAA stock-car competition in 1955 thanks to the factory-sponsored efforts of Carl Kiekhaefer's Mercury Outboards racing team. On the NASCAR circuit, Tim Flock won 13 consecutive Grand National races at the wheel of his Kiekhaefer 300 on the way to copping the season title. Another Kiekhaefer Chrysler, driven by Frank Mundy, won the AAA crown. In all, Chrysler 300s won 37 stock-car races in 1955.

Studebaker President Speedster

While not nearly as pricey as Packard's

Standard Speedster power was supplied by Studebaker's 185-horsepower, 259-cubic-inch V-8, which featured a four-barrel carburetor and dual exhausts. Buyers had a choice between a three-speed manual transmission with overdrive or the Automatic Drive automatic.

Caribbean convertible, Chrysler's luxurious 300 was still well beyond the reach of most performance buyers in 1955. But if an exclusive, sporty flair was the goal, and you were willing to spend halfway between Chevy's Hot One and Chrysler's best, Studebaker had the car for you—that is if you also liked big, chrome-encrusted bumpers and "tri-level" paint schemes.

Priced at $3253, Studebaker's President Speedster was, in the long-time wagon-maker's own words, "designed to appeal particularly to owners who desire special sports-car styling and performance with traditional American car comfort." The sporty Speedster did this trick for one year only, disappearing once Studebaker's Hawks landed in 1956.

The '55 President Speedster's body was the same basic shell Bob Bourke had created in Raymond Loewy's studio for Studebaker's classic '53 Starliner

coupe. Bourke's work would end up carrying over far longer than Studebaker originally intended, due to budget limitations. That that same basic body did so for nearly a decade stood as testament to its almost timeless beauty. That that beauty was almost lost beneath the styling makeover applied in 1955 very nearly left the joke on Studebaker. As one critic in the automotive press put it, the '55 Studes looked like "a chrome-happy kid had a holiday."

More chrome up front. More chrome on the sides. More chrome on top. Beyond that, the President Speedster also added two large, chromed foglamps up front as standard equipment. Also included in the standard package was a wide chrome band over the roof, directly in front of the rear window. Simulated wire wheel covers were thrown in as well, as was that intriguing tri-level paint scheme. Done in such shades as pink and gray

Studebaker was always at the cutting edge as far as sporty interior design was concerned in the '50s. Included in the Speedster deal was an engine-turned instrument panel with a 160-mile-per-hour speedometer, 8000-rpm tach, and full instrumentation. The round, black "plug" on the floor is a transmission inspection port cover.

Even more flashy than Studebaker's President Speedster was Packard's Caribbean convertible, which in 1955 and 1956 received a true triple-tone paint scheme. The twin hood scoops and aerials were also part of the package, as was a dual-carb V-8.

or lemon and lime, the Speedster's exterior featured a "sandwich" of color with one shade used for the roof and lower body sides, the other for the hood, deck lid, fender tops, and atop the doors.

Inside was a definitely sporty, diamond-quilted leather/vinyl interior color-keyed to at least attempt to match the exterior. The dash featured an engine-turned instrument panel incorporating full instrumentation, including a 160-mile-per-hour speedometer and an 8000-rpm tach. Additional standard features included power steering and brakes, a clock, and a radio. Standard power came from Studebaker's 259-cubic-inch overhead-valve V-8, which produced 185

horsepower with a four-barrel and dual exhausts. Behind that V-8 was either a three-speed manual with overdrive or the Automatic Drive auto trans.

Road-testing an Automatic Drive Speedster, *Motor Life*'s Ken Fermoyle reported that the 0–60 run could be made in 10 seconds flat, but only with a little creative shifting. Overall, Fermoyle was impressed by the special-edition sportster. "Lively is the word for the Studebaker Speedster," he wrote, "both in appearance and performance. For the past few years many automobile fanciers have wondered why Studebaker didn't supply a little more urge in the engine compartment to go with

the beautiful and distinctive styling of its cars. Those who felt this way should be very happy with the new Speedster."

Motor Trend's testers were equally impressed. In their opinion, the Speedster was "fun to drive, both from a performance and handling standpoint. It should make an ideal automobile for anyone who wants a car with semi-sports car characteristics and a 'different' appearance, but who needs room for four or five people. The many custom touches and 'extras' which are ordinarily added cost items—power steering, power brakes, special paint job—combine to make it a high performer ideal for family driving."

Few families found the chance to experience Studebaker's President Speedster, as only 2,215 were built. But if you did miss that opportunity in 1955, much of the Speedster's sporty pizzazz and performance was recaptured by Studebaker's Golden Hawk in 1956.

That, however, was another year. And another story.

LEFT
Packard's 275-horsepower, 352-cubic-inch V-8 was fed by two Rochester four-barrel carburetors. Behind it was the company's new Twin-Ultramatic automatic transmission, created by a young engineer named John Z. DeLorean. Dual exhausts were also standard Caribbean fare in 1955.

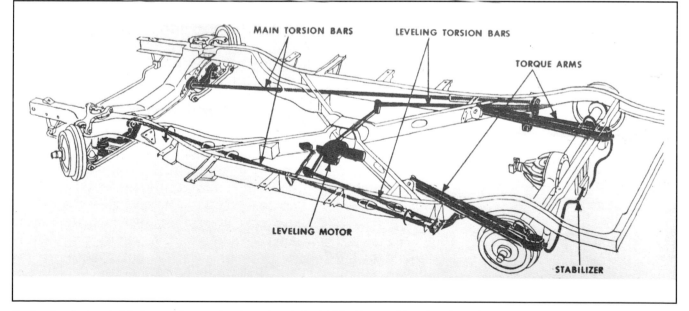

Packard rolled out this innovative torsion-bar chassis in 1955. Along with tying front and rear wheel action together, this design also featured a self-levelling system. An electric leveling motor automatically twisted the bars to increase spring tension whenever the car was loaded down.

5

THE REST OF THE STORY
Detroit's Horsepower Race Really Heats Up

AMERICAN car buyers who had started feeling the heat in 1955 soon found themselves in need of some serious relief beginning in 1956. Once Chevrolet had given the power to the people, there was no stopping the rest of Detroit from retaliating with even more and more muscle. Horsepower levels in the second half of the decade threatened to go off the scale. And the way in which the various automakers fought back helped change completely the way U.S. car buyers looked at the packages their horsepower came in. Before 1955, the American performance automobile was a loosely defined animal. For the most part during the first half of the decade, a factory hot rod's identity was given away only by the number of horses found hiding beneath the hood. The muscle was there, on a relative scale, but the muscle T-shirts weren't. Exceptions—Nash-Healey, Corvette, and Packard Caribbean—were few and extremely hard to come by

That situation began to change, however slightly, in 1955 when Ed Cole's Bow-Tie boys put a truly attractive, definitely modern body atop its little Hot One—no particularly special performance identification, just enough up-to-date sex appeal to prove that budget-minded customers could look good and go fast, too. But just for grins, there were those twin exhaust trumpets and two little "V" badges in back, one below each taillight, to let a stoplight challenger know just what type of beast had just had his lunch.

A sporty utility vehicle in any form, Chevrolet's Nomad station wagon turned into a true dazzler in 1957 when equipped with optional fuel injection, which was available for any model, even the mundane sedan delivery.

On the other side of the coin, there was no denying—no way, no how—the presence of Studebaker's brand of sporty performance in 1955. If you missed the President Speedster you needed to check your pulse. In between the "Eat at Joe's" Stude and Chevy's Motoramic motivator was Chrysler's beautiful, brutish 300, probably Detroit's first modern ancestor of the musclecar breed to follow in the '60s. The C-300 had the panache, the pomposity, and the power. It all was in there; this big boulevard cruiser looked and felt every bit as hot as it ran.

With such precedents established, it was soon no-holds-barred as Detroit's horsepower race headed down the homestretch on its mad dash into the '60s. From 1956 on, both performance and performance imagery became prominent selling points across the board in the Motor City, far more so than ever before.

The Hot One Gets Hotter

It's only right to begin the late '50s tale of the tape with Chevrolet, since it was Chevy that first put so much performance into the hands of so many drivers in exchange for so few dollars. Cole's kids just couldn't stop playing with fire after 1955, they came right back in 1956 with even more power for the people who preferred seeing the U.S.A. quickly in a Chevrolet.

"The Hot One's Even Hotter," claimed Chevy advertisements for 1956. Inspiration for this ad came from the company's latest and greatest Turbo-Fire 265 V-8, a 205-horsepower screamer that made the Power Pack 265 from 1955 look like a lukewarm loper in comparison. A four-barrel carb, dual exhausts, and a boost to 9.25:1 compression helped make the 1956 Turbo-Fire V-8 what it was. Also assisting was a new

Chevy offered two versions of the fuel-injected 283 V-8 in 1957. With a hydraulic cam, fuelie output was 250 horsepower. Armed with the fabled solid-lifter "Duntov" cam, the injected engine produced one horsepower per cubic inch—283 horsepower.

cam "with characteristics that would spell full race in large letters if seen a couple of years ago," according to *Motor Life*. "Duration of this frightening valve tickler is a healthy 270 degrees as against 252 degrees for the cam in the regular run," continued that March 1956 report. "Even though a fairly long ramp cuts down valve acceleration and takes some of the pepper out of the cam, these characteristics make it a very hot stick indeed, ramp or no ramp."

Even more interesting was the fact that this hot stick was a hydraulic unit, as were the cams used in all Chevy passenger-car V-8s, at least early in the year. The top Power Pack engine of 1955 made its 180 horsepower with a maintenance-intensive solid-lifter cam, as did all V-8s mated to manual transmissions. But this led to various over-revving maladies as many stick-shift buyers eagerly tested the Hot One's sky-high rpm limits, roughly 7000 revolutions in top tune. As *Motor Life* explained, "At speeds allowed by the solid tappets the rocker studs popped out like champagne corks at a Polish wedding." Of course, your studs would pop out, too, if you were turned over at 7000rpm.

Hydraulic lifters, due to their pump-up nature, inherently limit rpm. In over-simplified terms, things sorta stopped working once the oil pressure inside a hydraulic lifter pumped up beyond a certain level at a certain rev count. In the Super Turbo-Fire V-8's case, that count was roughly 6800 rpm, comfortably within this high-winder's safe limits, and well beyond the engine's usable power range in stone-stock applications. Anyone wanting any more revs than that would've been better advised to trade wheels for wings.

Firmly planted on the ground, Chevrolet's revised Turbo-Fire quickly impressed all critics with its ability to counter-rotate the planet beneath its wheels. Supplied with a '56 205-horsepower Chevy fitted with a three-speed and a 3.70:1 rear axle, *Road & Track*'s

test crew watched as that car hit 60 miles per hour in 9 seconds, the far end of the quarter in 16.16 seconds, and 111 miles per hour on the speedometer's right side. Was it any wonder *Mechanix Illustrated*'s Uncle Tom McCahill called the 1956 Turbo-Fire Chevrolet "the best performance buy in the world?" In his humble opinion, the hot, new Chevy "would whiz by a Duesenberg like Halley's Comet, [and] the vacuum as it went by would suck the stork off a Hispano-Suiza."

And to think this wasn't even the hottest Bow-Tie passenger-car product offered in 1956.

Just before the annual Speed Weeks trials in Florida in February, Chevrolet announced it would be dropping the Corvette's top V-8 beneath 1956 passenger-line hoods. Like its Bel Air brother, the optional Corvette powerplant featured 9.25:1 compression. But the sports-car V-8 had a solid-lifter cam, larger ports, and two four-barrel carbs flowing about 375 cfm each. Maximum output was 225 horsepower at 5200 rpm, more than enough fuel for Uncle Tom's analogy-o-matic machine.

As McCahill saw it, the 225-horsepower Chevrolet represented "a poor man's answer to a hot Ferrari." Once suitably warmed up, he continued to color the image. "Here's an engine that can wind up tighter than the E-string on an East Laplander's mandolin, well beyond 6000 rpm without blowing up like a pigeon egg in a shotgun barrel," he wrote. "Zero to 30 averages 3.2 seconds, 0–60 8.9 seconds, and in 12 seconds, you're doing 70. This is just about May, June and July faster than the Chevrolets of just two or three years ago." The hottest Chevy V-8 yet, he concluded, "might very well be rated the greatest competition engine ever built."

On the sands at Daytona in February 1956, one '56 Chevy reached 136 miles per hour, only to be disqualified from an official record after "mysteriously" shedding its fan belt, a supposedly unfortunate mishap that instantly freed an estimated 15-25 horses from the mundane tasks of cooling the engine and generating electricity. What could've Duntov's guys been thinking?

In 1957, Chevrolet engineers bored out the 265 to 283 cubic inches and created a complete line-up of even hotter V-8s, with two versions of the "2x4" option offered, one at 245 horsepower, the other at 270. Of course, the really big news involved the introduction of Ramjet fuel injection for the 283. It, too, came in two forms, 250 horsepower with a hydraulic lifters, 283 with the tried-and-true solid-lifter "Duntov cam."

Designers the following year bulked up the next new Chevrolet in keeping with a corporate trend towards the "bigger must be better" ideal. And to help celebrate the arrival of the division's fourth restyled new model in four years, Chevy's image-conscious crew also rolled out the company's first truly special special-edition model, the Impala, offered both in

The twin, bright exhaust tips below the rear bumper on this Bel Air hardtop mean there's more beneath the hood than the standard 265 V-8. In 1956, Chevrolet claimed "the Hot One's even hotter," inspired by the new 205hp 265 V-8. Then in February 1956, Chevrolet announced even more power would become available as the Corvette's dual-carb V-8 would be listed as a passenger car option. This '56 Chevy is one of the first models so equipped.

Fed by twin Carter four-barrels, this Chevy V-8 produced 225 horsepower thanks to a serious cam and 9.25:1 compression. In 1957, a 283-cubic-inch, dual-carb V-8 would appear with 245 horses. Trading its hydraulic cam for a solid-lifter unit helped bump output to 270 horsepower.

sexy sport coupe and desirable drop-top forms. Being that these totally redesigned '58 Chevys were longer, wider, and heavier—some of the weight coming by way of a liberal coat of chrome—it was only natural that a bigger, stronger, and sturdier V-8 appear to better help carry the load.

That engine was the 348-cubic-inch "W-head" V-8, nicknamed for its zig-zag valve layout. Borrowed from the company's truck line, the 348 was modified for passenger-car applications only as a performance mill—nothing short of a four-barrel carburetor and cutting-edge high compression were ever included as part of the mix. Impressive enough in its day on its own, the 348's main claim to fame was its foundation-laying status; in 1961, it was redesigned into the legendary 409, a truly hot performance mill that had everyone singing its praises that year.

Three years before, the 348 was producing 250 horsepower in top four-barrel tune and a healthy 280 horses with Chevy's new "3x2" induction system featuring a trio of Rochester two-barrel carburetors. Offered again in 1959, the top triple-carb 348 was rated at 315 horsepower. And for the first time, a Chevrolet passenger car could've been factory ordered that year with a modern floor-shifted four-speed, equipment any self-respecting musclecar man wouldn't be caught dead without just a few short years later. While four-speeds were making their debut, fuel injection was fading out from the passenger-car ranks. Both were extremely rare options in 1959.

Oldsmobile's J-2 Rocket V-8

Chevrolet wasn't alone, among GM's divisions, in heating up the late '50s by introducing exotic induction equipment. In 1957, Oldsmobile rolled out its J-2 option, available on any model, two-door or four-door, for only $83. Stars of the J-2 show were three

two-barrel carburetors controlled by a progressive linkage. Atop Olds' 371-cubic-inch V-8 (with 10:1 compression instead of the standard 9.5:1), the J-2 equipment upped output from 277 horsepower to 300. While some critics felt that figure wasn't quite what you might expect from an engine of such large proportions, they couldn't deny the J-2 V-8's ability to uproot stumps and melt rubber. Maximum torque output was a then-whopping 412 pounds-feet at 2800 rpm.

Even more J-2 muscle was offered by way of an extremely rare "off-road" version intended for racers only. Rated at 312 horsepower, this track-ready, limited-availability J-2 package was reportedly priced at $395.

On the street, a big, luxurious J-2 Olds 98 did 0–60 in 9.1 seconds in a *Motor Trend* road test. Obviously, the lighter 88 models with the tri-carb V-8 promised even lower numbers, undoubtedly well into the 8-second range. And fitted one more time within the larger, heavier '58 models, Oldsmobile's J-2 Rocket V-8 was still a force to reckoned with, even if it was well hidden beneath all that blinding chrome.

Running right along with Oldsmobile's J-2 in 1957 was Pontiac's similar setup, equipment literally copied right out from under Olds engineers noses. By 1957, Bunkie Knudsen's Pontiac Motor Division was making some serious performance noises as Oldsmobile refugee Pete Estes' engineering team was busy spitting out hot hardware seemingly by the bushel-basket load. Hotter cams, courtesy of long-time grind expert Malcolm "Mac" McKellar, increasingly larger V-8s, and beefed driveline pieces were just the beginning.

Pontiac's Tri Power V-8

Not long after Olds released its J-2 option, Pontiac also stuck three Rochester two-barrel carbs atop a special intake for its 347-cubic-inch V-8 early in 1957. Equipped for the street with 10:1 compression and hydraulic lifters, the Tri Power 347 V-8 produced 290 maximum horses at 5000 rpm. Racing-inspired versions were rated at 317 horsepower.

More compression and another displacement increase (to 370 cubic inches) helped bump optional Tri Power output to 300 horsepower in 1958; yet more cubes (389) in 1959 unleashed yet more triple-carb horses, 315. Race-ready examples were rated at 330 horsepower in 1958, 345 in 1959. That GM wasn't supposed to be supplying racers with such weapons, per the 1957 AMA mandate, was apparently of little concern to Bunkie, Pete, and the boys. By 1960, Pontiac would be beating all comers severely about the head and shoulders, on superspeedways and at the drags.

Pontiac Bonneville

Pontiac people were also responsible for one of the '50s more prominent high-powered image

Studebaker's Golden Hawk picked up where the President Speedster left off in 1955. Inside was a sporty interior reminding many of what the Speedster had offered. Meanwhile, beneath the '56 Golden Hawk's hood was Packard's big 352-cubic-inch V-8.

LEFT
With a single four-barrel carburetor and dual exhausts, the Golden Hawk's 352 V-8 rated 275 horsepower, enough muscle to help produce 0 to 60 times in the eight-second range. On the flipside, the engine was quite large (725 pounds), meaning the Golden Hawk was very nose heavy. Handling suffered accordingly. In this case, the chrome valve covers are missing their standard engine identification decals.

Inside, a '56 D500 model (the package was available for all bodystyles—convertibles, station wagons, etc.) was all stock Dodge; nothing more, nothing less. Notice the automatic transmission pushbutton controls to the left of the steering wheel.

LEFT
Unlike Plymouth and DeSoto, which both unleashed high-profile, limited-edition performance machines in 1956, Dodge officials opted for a no-nonsense approach. Their D500 option simply put the customer's money to use where it worked best—beneath the hood and at all four wheels. Along with a 315-cubic-inch hemi V-8, the D500 option included bigger brakes and a stiffer suspension, equipment that came in handy on NASCAR tracks.

machines, a breed first created in 1955 by Chrysler with its C-300. Sorry, Packard fans, although the Caribbean convertible of 1953 was indeed an exclusive, image-conscious offering with ample horsepower, its antiquated L-head straight-eight left it a bit lacking when compared to the high-winding V-8s from Cadillac and Lincoln. And Chrysler's C-300 was ready, willing, and able to dominate everyone in the luxury-performance market by the time the

The D500's 315-cubic-inch hemi V-8 featured a solid-lifter cam, 9.25:1 compression, dual exhausts, and a single Carter WCFB four-barrel carburetor. The chrome valve covers are non-stock, owner-installed features.

Caribbean was fitted with its first modern overhead-valve V-8 in 1955.

As for Pontiac's variation on the luxury hot rod theme, in February 1957 Knudsen proudly watched as his division unveiled its Bonneville convertible, the first of many Pontiac automobiles to borrow famous racing names to imply an image of prolific performance. Le Mans (guilty only by association), Grand Prix (more luxury than performance), GTO (definitely racy), and Trans Am (even more so) would later follow.

Specially trimmed and loaded to the grille with luxury and convenience options, the long, low, limited-edition Bonneville convertible was priced at $5782, more than $2500 above the bottom line for a typical Star Chief drop-top in 1957. Included for that bank-breaking asking price was a fuel-injected 347-cubic-inch V-8, an engine created exclusively for the Bonneville image. It suited that image well, what with its 310 horses and 400 pounds-feet of torque, ample oomph to push this 4285-pound showboat to the forefront of this country's passenger-car performance scene in 1957.

Compared to its Tri Power counterpart, which could reportedly do the quarter mile in 16.8 seconds, the injected Bonneville convertible, with all its extra poshness and weight, was considerably slower at the strip (18 seconds). But almost in defiance of physical laws, the big, luxurious Bonneville could reach 60 miles per hour from rest in an amazing 8.1 seconds—bigger in this case did mean better.

After building only 630 fuel-injected Bonneville convertibles in 1957, Pontiac watered down the image the following year, moving the tricky injection gear to the options list and adding a hardtop version. Production was 9144 for the '58 Bonneville hardtop and 3096 for its topless counterpart. For 1959, the Bonneville's exclusive image was diversified even further, and its days as one of GM's top performers ended completely.

Ford Thunderbird

As for Ford Motor Company, it basically steered clear of the late '50s performance scene after giving up on its supercharged and dual-carbureted 312 early in 1957 once the AMA factory racing ban was announced. Sure, Lincoln and Mercury introduced massive engines and triple carburetors late in the decade, but these options came about simply in order to help better motivate the incredibly large bodies that had begun piling on top in 1958.

Ford's once-spritely Thunderbird also bulked up almost beyond recognition in 1958, forever leaving behind any misunderstandings concerning its identity. Many Detroit-watchers before that year had considered the two-seat T-birds to be quasi-sports cars, often comparing them to definitely sporty rivals from Chevrolet and Studebaker. And in 1957, almost as many witnesses felt there was more to come in the way of American sports-car performance.

Predicting just such a future, *Motor Trend*'s Wayne Thoms had this to say in the August 1957 issue: "If there are to be more Detroit sports cars, we hope they'll embody some of the principles learned from the instrumentation of the Golden Hawk, the cornering ability of the Corvette, and the detail finish of the Thunderbird."

Studebaker Golden Hawk

The Golden Hawk Thoms spoke of was Studebaker's latest sporty rendition of the lovely "Loewy coupe" first introduced in 1953. Following in the '55 Speedster's tire tracks, the '56 Golden Hawk offered room for five, along with an exclusive air and the highest level of performance Studebaker could offer. Exclusivity was supplied by a deluxe interior and various trim baubles, the most notable being a pair of add-on fiberglass fins mounted atop those beautiful rear quarters Raymond Loewy's

DeSoto's limited-edition Adventurer hardtop was offered in either black or white, with both colors complemented considerably by gold accents. Exclusive power came from a 320-horsepower, 341-cubic-inch hemi V-8. *Courtesy Chrysler Historical*

design team (Robert Bourke, to be exact) had originally fashioned in 1953.

Although not nearly as obvious as its Speedster forerunner, the '56 Golden Hawk did, nonetheless, portray a Euro-style sporty image in fine fashion, most of that fashion coming inside. Picking up where the Speedster left off, the Golden Hawk also featured a bright, engine-turned instrument panel with full instrumentation, including a tachometer and vacuum gauge.

At the other end of that gauge was Packard's 352-cubic-inch V-8, an engine that was every bit as heavy (725 pounds) as it was strong. Output with a single four-barrel feeding fuel and air was 275 horses. But while all this Packard power did help the '56 Golden Hawk record impressive 0–60 times in the 8-second range, the additional pounds created a pronounced forward weight bias. At best, overall handling was above average compared to typical American cars, but a bit lacking up against the agile Corvette and reasonably spry T-bird.

How much this nose-heavy bias actually harmed handling varies by account. The bottom line, however, was that the car did display a distinct understeer tendency, as well as an inherent ability to spin the rear tires into oblivion when the throttle was mashed with authority. After melting the rubber beneath his test Golden Hawk during acceleration runs, Tom McCahill explained that, "If I'd shoved 200 or 300 pounds of sand in the trunk to equalize the weight distribution, my times would have been considerably better."

Studebaker engineers, of course, weren't interested in making a trunk-mounted sandbox optional equipment for the Golden Hawk. But they could make changes elsewhere to better balance the car.

When the '57 Golden Hawk appeared, with the same sporty interior, it featured new steel rear fins and an add-on "power bulge" atop its hood. New as well was overall performance. In *Hot Rod*'s words, the revamped 1957 edition was "as far removed from its '56 namesake as it is from a Sherman tank." Most importantly, it could "cut a pretty fancy corner without any of the front end 'wash out' displayed by the '56."

How did Studebaker-Packard's people do it? For starters, they got the car's weight distribution back to more acceptable levels by using a lighter engine. Luckily, the big 352 Packard V-8 went out of production after 1956, leaving engineers to make do with Studebaker's proven "Sweepstakes" 289-cubic-inch V-8. About 100 pounds lighter than the Packard engine, the Sweepstakes 289 was also less powerful at 210 horsepower. Engineers, however, had a solution for that problem, too.

Standard equipment on all 4,356 Golden Hawks built for 1957 was McCulloch's ever-present power-boosting supercharger, the same belt-driven blower used by Ford that year. Stuffing five pounds of maximum air pressure into the 289's carburetor, the McCulloch supercharger helped Studebaker's smaller V-8 put out as many horses as its big Packard cousin—275. Both the horsepower-per-cubic-inch and pounds-per-horsepower ratios for the Golden Hawk were among the industry's highest in 1957. This translated into a 0–60 in 7.46 seconds and a top speed of 127.5 miles per hour for *Speed Age*'s test driver Bob Veith. That same test produced a 6.93/122.5 score for the Corvette, 8.49/119.3 for the Thunderbird.

Exclusivity was key in the case of Plymouth's first pure performance offering. All '56 Fury models were hardtops with Eggshell White paint complemented by gold anodized accents. Underpinnings were typically heavy-duty and power was plentiful.

"The supercharged engine makes the Golden Hawk a hard car to pass on the straightaway," concluded Wayne Thoms. Studebaker came back with basically the same package, save for a switch to smaller 14-inch wheels, in 1958, a year when customers apparently found it easy to pass on the supercharged Golden Hawk. Only 878 were built. Non-supercharged Hawks would end up carrying the Studebaker performance banner into the '60s.

Another 588 Packard Hawks were created in 1958, they with their odd, grafted-on snout and large hood scoop. Beneath that scoop was still a standard supercharged 289, making this Packard variation every bit as strong a performer as its Studebaker counterpart. But neither were tough enough to carry their company's fortunes for long. Packard models themselves were history after 1958. The Studebaker-Packard name survived until 1962, while the Studebaker half of the equation finally left the U.S. for Canada in 1963. Studebaker cars ceased to exist after 1966.

AMC Rambler Rebel

Far less well-known, but every bit as quick as the supercharged Golden Hawks, was another special-edition performance model introduced in 1957. It, too, was from an independent automaker, this one far more healthier than Studebaker-Packard. The company was AMC, home of Nash and Hudson before those long-standing, once-respected nameplates were unceremoniously dropped after 1957. AMC fooled everyone that year with its Rambler Rebel, a Corvette-killer that came and went so quick it basically never got the chance to show Chevy fans what-for. They would've never known what had hit them, anyway.

For starters, the car was a Rambler, supposedly an affordable, practical, down-sized line aimed at capturing a new market then developing strongly in this country—that is, the affordable, practical, down-sized niche. Additionally, the Rebel was a four-door hardtop, not exactly a model you'd expect to see squared off up against a fiberglass two-seater.

Yet there was the Rebel, with its heavy-duty chassis featuring beefed springs, stiff Gabriel shocks, and a stabilizer bar at each end. Power steering and brakes were standard, as was AMC's big, new 327-cubic-inch overhead-valve V-8, rated at 255 real horses. Weighing only 3,350 pounds, the '57 Rebel could brag of an excellent power-to-weight ratio of 13 pounds per

Additional exclusive treatment carried over inside the '56 Fury, where door panels and seats were treated to special "herring-bone" upholstery.

RIGHT
Fury power came from a 303-cubic-inch V-8 offered only under those Eggshell White hoods. Like all its rivals, this powerplant featured high compression (9.25:1), a special high-lift cam, and dual low-restriction exhausts. A single four-barrel carburetor handled fuel/air metering. Output was 240 horsepower.

Although it looked very much like DeSoto's Adventurer, this '56 Indy pace car replica is basically a standard Fireflite convertible with Adventurer trim—all special-edition '56 Adventurers were hardtops. DeSoto officially introduced the pace car convertible replicas in January 1956; the Adventurer hardtop emerged five weeks later.

horsepower. This ratio might have been even more dominating had AMC engineers followed through on their promise to equip the Rebel's 327 V-8 with Bendix fuel injection. That result would've in turn depended on the Bendix unit's promise to do its job as advertised. Apparently none did, as Chrysler performance buyers in 1958 would discover.

Though the fuel-injected 327 never made it into production, the Rebel did receive a heavy dose of exclusive image treatment. On the outside, silver paint was complemented by large, gold-anodized body-side trim (with "Rebel" script up front), and a Continental spare-tire mount—optional for other Rambler hardtops—was standard in back. Also standard was a padded dash and sun visors inside. Price for the whole works was only $2,786, making the Rebel easily one of the best performance buys of its day—or many other days for that matter.

While the '56 Adventurer hardtop received a 320-horsepower, 341-cubic-inch hemi, the Indy pacer convertibles were all fitted with the smaller 255-horsepower, 330-cubic-inch hemi.

Most would never have glanced twice at the AMC Rebel in 1957, at least not if a performance car was what they sought. But this four-door hardtop was one of the hottest cars of its day thanks to a dominating power-to-weight ratio. *Courtesy Chrysler Historical and Publications International, Chicago*

Most innocent bystanders would've probably never guessed that the Rambler Rebel could run from 0 to 60 miles per hour in about 7.5 seconds. Or hit 115 miles per hour on top end. As auto journalist Joe Wherry explained, "That is high performance, believe me, when family cars are under discussion." Hey, Joe, that is high performance when any car is under discussion. Then or now.

Its image was obviously exclusive. Its edition was definitely limited—only 1500 were built. And its performance was certainly hot. But its overall impressions—those off just another family man's four-door hardtop—didn't do much for the Rambler Rebel's ability to wow the masses in 1957. Today, very few performance followers even remember such an animal ever existed.

Chrysler Performance

The same will never be said about Chrysler, hands down the king of the limited-edition, high-profile performance scene in the late '50s. Chrysler Corporation truly took wing in 1956 after shocking the troops the year before with the C-300 luxury bombshell. Along with rolling out an even more powerful 300 letter-car in 1956, the corporation also unveiled similarly hot, exclusive performance packages for each of its lesser divisions—DeSoto, Dodge, and Plymouth. In respective order, these attractive performers were the Adventurer, D-500, and Fury.

For Dodge, high-profile performance wasn't anything all that new; its Red Ram hemi V-8 had been offering some of the industry's meanest muscle for a couple years up to that point. For DeSoto, however,

the appearance in 1956 of bawdy, 300-type performance was a bit of eye-opener, even though it, too, had been enjoying hefty hemi horsepower since 1952. But in Plymouth's case, the introduction of an honest-to-goodness factory hot rod sounded almost too good to be true.

Plymouth Fury

Two years before, Plymouths were about as dull and practical as it got in the American automobile arena: boring, dated styling and antiquated L-head six-cylinder power—a truly tired image. Then came 1955 and a total redesign. Overnight, the Plymouth was pretty and powerful, the latter thanks to its first overhead-valve V-8, the 260-cubic-inch poly-head. Though not nearly as hot as its all-new rival from Chevrolet, the '55 Plymouth was no slouch. And it was a start.

Plymouth's movers and shakers showed they knew a little bit about lighting fires themselves in 1956. Hot performance was what the new Fury was all about. Introduced at the Chicago Auto Show on January 10 that year, Plymouth's attractive, limited-edition performer came standard with a larger, 303-cubic-inch V-8 borrowed from the Canadian Chrysler line. Inside went domed 9.25:1 pistons and a special high-lift cam. A four-barrel carburetor metered fuel and air, while low-restriction dual exhausts handled spent gases. Output for this package was 240 horsepower. Behind this engine was a heavy-duty clutch and a three-speed manual, with the pushbutton-controlled two-speed Powerflite automatic available at extra cost.

Stiffer springs and shocks and a larger stabilizer bar typically suspended the Fury. Brakes were 11-inch Dodge drums, and tires were big 7.10-inch treads on 15-inch wheels.

American Motors' surprising Rebel hardtop drew its strength from this 327-cubic-inch V-8. Fed by a single four-barrel carb, this engine pumped out 255 horses. Optional Bendix fuel injection was originally offered, but quickly withdrawn before any examples were built. *Courtesy Chrysler Historical and Publications International, Chicago*

ABOVE

n 1957, Studebaker traded the big, burly Packard V-8 for its own "Sweepstakes" 289 cubic inch V-8, a smaller powerplant that helped make the second-edition Golden Hawk a better handler in the turns. To compensate for the loss of both cubes and horses, a McCulloch supercharger was added. All Golden Hawks built in 1957 and 1958 came standard with the McCulloch blower, as did all Packard Hawks produced in 1958.

On top, the first Fury was as unique-looking as it was powerful. To set it apart from the crowd, a gold-anodized treatment was applied to the grille, wheel covers, and in wide swathe down each side. Complementing the gold trim was Eggshell White paint; the only color available for the Fury.

That exclusive golden Fury image continued for 1957, with fresh Exner styling accentuating the package. New for that year was a slightly different exterior finish featuring Buckskin Beige paint. Meanwhile, beneath the hood was a new powerplant, the 318-

With the McCulloch-supplied belt-driven blower delivering five pounds of maximum boost, the smaller Studebaker V-8 could produce the same 275 horsepower created by the bigger Packard engine it replaced.

cubic-inch Dual Fury V-800. Heavy-duty from top to bottom, the Fury's latest V-8 was now fed by two Carter four-barrel carburetors. Output listed at 290 horsepower. And with Chrysler's innovative chassis, featuring torsion bars up front, the second-edition Fury probably handled as well as any performance passenger car in the '50s.

Fury production reached 7438 for 1957, compared to 4485 the previous year. Another 5303 similarly gold-dusted models rolled out in 1958, most with the 290-horsepower 318 engine. Others featured yet another new power source, the optional Golden Commando V-8. Priced at $324, the Golden Commando displaced 350 cubic inches and was rated at 305 horsepower. Golden Commando engines, like all Chrysler's top performance mills that year, could've also been fitted—for an additional $500 or so—with Bendix fuel injection. Once more, the few that were originally fuel injected ended up retrofitted with dual fours once the realities of the troublesome Bendix injection system were discovered.

As has so often been the case in Detroit, Plymouth's originally exclusive Fury legacy was completely watered down after 1958, with the name being applied to an entire model line in 1959. At least there was a special sub-series at the top, the aptly named Sport Fury.

For starters, the '59 Sport Fury was only offered as a two-door hardtop or convertible. Nowhere was the "Sport Fury" name actually used on the outside, but the premium-line Plymouth, nonetheless, was not easy to miss. Large silver-anodized trim ran down the body sides. Inside that trim in back was golden "Fury" script. Above and behind that script was a dramatic medallion containing Exner's "Forward Look" logo. That same logo appeared in the grille, while Exner's pet styling cue, the "sport deck lid tire cover," also came standard.

Base engine was the Fury V-800 with Super Pak—a 318-cubic-inch V-8 with high-lift cam; 9:1 compression; large-diameter, free-flowing dual exhausts; and a Carter AFB (aluminum four-barrel) carburetor. In Sport Fury tune, the V-800 Super Pak produced 260 horsepower and 345 pounds-feet of

The exclusive color used for Plymouth's Fury was changed to Buckskin Beige in 1957. All that gold trim, however, remained in place. *Courtesy Chrysler Historical*

In 1957 and 1958, standard power for the Plymouth Fury was supplied by the "Dual Fury V-800" engine, a 318-cubic-inch dual-carb V-8 rated at 290 horsepower. The exclusive gold-accented Fury exterior carried over, then was discontinued after 1958.

RIGHT
Although its basic body shape was still tied to Pontiac's "old man's car" past, the '57 models featured much more power beneath the skin. Early in the year, PMD engineers announced the arrival of the optional Tri Power equipment for the 347-cubic-inch V-8. Featuring three two-barrel carburetors, the Tri Power setup helped boost output to 290 horses. No external identification was used in 1957; in 1958, very noticeable "Tri Power" badges were added to the front fenders.

torque. For $74 more, a Sport Fury buyer could take control of the Golden Commando 395 V-8. Though the golden Fury image had dimmed on the outside, the mother lode could still be had under the hood. Both valve covers and the special open-element air cleaner on the Golden Commando 395 were painted gold.

Those who chose the Golden Commando also hit the jackpot in the power department. With 10:1 compression, a Carter AFB carb, high-lift cam, and special low-restriction dual exhausts, the 361-cubic-inch V-8 pumped out 305 horsepower and turned out 395 pounds-feet of torque—thus the engine's name.

Other than the Golden Commando 395, perhaps the most noticeable Sport Fury feature for 1959 was found inside the passenger compartment. "Never before has the low-price field seen a costly car feature like the Sport Fury's standard equipment swivel front seats," bragged sales brochures. "At the touch of a finger, front seats swing to face the curb. Sit down, then swivel to face front again." Sport Fury models in 1959 were also guaranteed an exclusive flair all their own thanks to a special dash plaque announcing that each car was "built especially for [your name here] by Plymouth." Plymouth inscribed more than 23,500 of these plaques in 1959.

Like the Fury, DeSoto's Adventurer also kept its high-profile golden exterior treatment in 1957. *Courtesy Chrysler Historical*

DeSoto Adventurer

DeSoto's Adventurer was itself introduced early in 1956 wearing an exclusive image quite similar to Plymouth's original Fury. Like the '56 Fury, the '56 Adventurer's exterior featured Eggshell White paint accentuated with golden complements, this time painted on the body sides and roof. Gold anodizing did appear on the grille and wheel covers. Unlike the Fury, the first Adventurer could also be painted black instead of white.

As expected, standard features abounded, including a heavy-duty suspension underneath. Beneath the hood, standard power came from a bored-out DeSoto hemi with a hot cam and 9.5:1 compression. Displacing 341 cubic inches, this hot hemi was rated at 320 horsepower. Backing up this engine was the two-speed Powerflite automatic transmission. Price for this exclusive DeSoto was enough to make potential customers think they were buying real gold. At $3,728, the '56 Adventurer hardtop was one of DeSoto's most expensive offerings up to that point. Only 996 were built, all sold within six weeks after introduction in February 1956.

Additionally, a special run of Indy 500 pace-car-replica convertibles were also built in 1956. Although these looked like Adventurer hardtops on the outside, they were basically standard Fireflite convertibles beneath the skin, with DeSoto's smaller, 255-horsepower 330 hemi V-8 residing under the hood.

Adventurer hardtop performance in 1956 was predictably impressive, what with all those hemi horses hauling that 3870-pound body around. Rest to 60 miles per hour took 10.5 seconds, the quarter mile needed 7 seconds more. At Daytona Beach that spring, a '56 Adventurer hit 137 miles per hour, performance later improved to 144 miles per hour at Chrysler's proving grounds in Chelsea, Michigan.

Even more performance potential was built in the following year with the arrival of the 345-horsepower 345-cubic-inch hemi as standard equipment for the '57 Adventurer. Also new that year was a true Adventurer convertible. Production was 1,650 hardtops and 300 convertibles. In 1958, Adventurer output remained at 345 horses, although that year the engine was a wedge-head instead of a hemi. Displacement was 361 cubic inches. Only 432 gold-trimmed DeSotos were sold in 1958, 82 of those convertibles. An even larger 383-cubic-inch wedge, rated at 350 horsepower, appeared the next year, the last for DeSoto's limited-edition cruiser in its original, exclusive form. Production was 590 coupes and 97 convertibles. Like Plymouth's Fury, the Adventurer name was then used for a typical model line-up in 1960.

Dodge D-500

Contrary to DeSoto and Plymouth's efforts, Dodge's hot performance package from the late '50s

Work on Oldsmobile's J-2 triple-carb design had commenced quite some time before assistant engineer Pete Estes had left his Olds position for the chief engineer's job at Pontiac. Thus, when Pontiac announced it would be offering a similar tri-carb option there was little doubt where the idea originated. With those three Rochester two-barrels feeding the flames, output for the 371-cubic-inch Olds Rocket V-8 went from 277 horsepower up to 300.

was a no-nonsense power package. Frills were not included. The D-500 option, introduced early in January 1956, put the buyer's money only where it counted—underneath at the wheels and between the fenders.

Priced at $125, the D-500 package started by adding bigger 12-inch brake drums with 2.5-inch-wide shoes—standard Dodge brakes were 11-inch drums with 2-inch-wide shoes. Stiffer springs (six leaves instead of five in back), shocks, and front stabilizer bar were, of course, also added. As for power, the D-500 used the 315-cubic-inch hemi V-8 with 9.25:1 compression, a special solid-lifter cam, and a single Carter WCFB four-barrel. Output was 260 horsepower. Interestingly, the D-500 performance option could've been added to any body style, two-door or four-door, hardtop, convertible, or station wagon. Best guesses put 1956 D-500 production, for all bodies, at perhaps 5000 or so.

Clearly, some serious horsepower was required to keep a '57 Oldsmobile up and running with the competition—these were big cars to say the least. While the Rocket V-8 was still no slouch, the J-2 option helped move things along a little more briskly.

And apparently, Dodge's brain trust in 1956 responded to pressures from buyers who wanted all that D-500 horsepower but didn't like the bigger brakes and rougher suspension. Some '56 D-500 Dodges came with the standard suspension and brakes. At the other end of the scale was the rare D-500-1, a rough-and-ready character fitted with a dual-carb hemi, reportedly rated at 295 horsepower. Estimates claim as many as 50 of these were built, with all them apparently done only in white. Why? Cop cars then were generally black on white. As the story goes, many of these D-500-1 Dodges were shipped to the California Highway Patrol, where patrolmen then found the cars to rough to live with.

In 1957, the D-500 option reappeared, this time with a 285-horsepower 325-cubic-inch hemi topped by a single Carter four-barrel. In reference to the 285-horsepower D-500 mill, *Sports Car Illustrated* felt it was "a well-balanced engine—not so big that it won't rev, and not so small that it lacks torque. As a result it delivers plenty of usable horsepower all the way up the line." Zero-to-60 for the '57 D-500 was listed at 8.5 seconds; 16.6 seconds at 83 miles per hour for the quarter mile.

Even wilder was a special run of D-501 Dodges, cars built with NASCAR racing and special-duty service in mind. Power for these brutes came from a 340-horsepower dual-carb 354 hemi borrowed from the Chrysler 300 arsenal. Everything about the D-501 Dodge was beefed, right down to its special 8-inch-wide wheels. No numbers are readily available, but those familiar with this race-bred breed believe about 100 may have been built in 1957.

Two street versions were listed the following year, the basic D-500 package with its single-carb 305-horsepower 361-cubic-inch wedge-head V-8, and the Super D-500 with dual fours and 320 horsepower. Also listed was a fuel-injected 361 rated at 333 horses. Again, the Bendix equipment never made it much past the break-in stage before being superseded by the twin-carb intake. Then, in 1959, Dodge's larger 383-cubic-inch wedge was substituted for the 361 in the D-500 deal. Base output that year, once more coming courtesy of a single Carter, was 320 horses. The Super D-500 383 with its dual Carters was rated at 345 horsepower. Dodge last offered the D-500 option in 1961. The only cars hotter from Chrysler Corporation in the late '50s were the big 300 letter cars.

Chrysler 300B

For 1956, Chrysler's 300B picked up right where the C-300 left off as "America's most power-

Pontiac entered the limited-edition performance car field in 1957, unveiling its impressive Bonneville convertible. Priced it an intimidating $5,782, the '57 Bonneville featured standard fuel-injected power. After building 630 Bonnevilles in 1957, Pontiac rolled out another 3096 in 1958. A hardtop model also appeared with production of that model totalling 9144. Fuel injection became an option in 1958. This Bonneville convertible is one of an estimated 400 to feature the F.I. engine that year.

Interestingly, Pontiac's fuel-injection equipment differed considerably in comparison to corporate cousin Chevrolet's. When mated to PMD's 347-cubic-inch V-8, this injection equipment helped up advertised output to 310 horsepower in 1957. In 1958, displacement jumped to 370 cubic inches while advertised output remained the same.

The '58 Bonneville was equipped with a sporty inerior with four individual bucket seats and gold fleck in the carpet—no, those many spots are not dirt.

ful production car." The body itself remained similar to the 1955 body. Up front, chrome headlight rings were exchanged for painted ones. In back, revised rear quarters, bumper, and taillights cleaned up the tail considerably. The biggest change came beneath the hood, where the 331 hemi was bored out to 354 cubic inches. While the twin four-barrels and high-lift cam carried over, compression was upped to 9:1, helping increase output to another industry high.

Standard 300B output was 340 horsepower, but that wasn't all. An optional 354 hemi with a compression boost to 10:1 was also offered, making the 300B Detroit's first member of the "one-horsepower-per-cubic-inch" club. No, Chevy fans, the Corvette wasn't the first American automobile to reach this coveted plateau. The 283-horsepower 283 fuel-injected V-8 came one year too late to earn that honor.

Again making its debut late, Chrysler's second-edition letter car was officially announced on January 4, 1956, then first appeared in public at the Chicago Auto Show two days later. Color choices remained limited to the three '55 finishes. But new options included air conditioning, the Highway Hi-Fi phonograph, and a self-winding clock mounted in the steering-wheel hub. Added, too, were two more transmissions, with the less-desirable Powerflite being joined by the exceptional, three-speed Torqueflite and a rare, beefed-up three-speed manual—only 31 stick-shift 300Bs were built. Handling was improved thanks to a set of standard Goodyear Blue Streak tires, and rear-axle ratio choices expanded to 12, with a brutish 6.17:1 stump-pulling rear end bringing up the bottom end.

"A mastodon of muscle,"was the typically humble description used by *Mechanix Illustrated*'s Tom McCahill. "Its very appearance," he wrote, "even when parked, gives the impression that [the 300B] is loaded with muscles, ready to spring into action the moment you flick the key." *Motorsport* magazine's testers clocked a 300B from rest to 60 miles per hour in 8.2 seconds. Quarter-mile performance also improved to 17 seconds at 84.1 miles per hour. According to *Motorsport*'s Bill Holland, "If you want to cruise slowly around town, [the 300B] isn't the car to buy. But if you can handle a fast car and want to go a long way in a hurry, this is your car." Traveling the flying mile in a hurry during the Daytona speed trials in February 1956, Tim Flock's 300B averaged 139.54 miles per hour, recording a one way high of 142.91.

Despite the 300B's impressive power, production for 1956 dropped to 1,060, with another 42 exported out of the country. But buyers who were perhaps tired of the car's styling found a new reason to check out Chrysler's luxury-performance model the following year.

Production of the third-edition 300 reached a high of 1,737 (along with 31 exports), undoubtedly thanks to a dazzling Virgil Exner restyle. Using a frontal design he first performed in clay on a 1955 model known as the "613," Exner produced a stunning, long, low, and sleek body for the '57 Chrysler line. Overall height was nearly 5 inches lower, body sides were even cleaner than previous models, and graceful, tasteful fins brought up the rear. Enhancing the long, low lines in 300 ranks was a convertible model, a first for the letter-car line. Only 484 drop-top 300Cs were built, with 479 of those delivered in the U.S. Prices were equally enhanced, as the convertible's bottom line started at $5400, the hardtop at around $5000.

123

Featuring the third all-new body in three years, Chevrolet's '59 Impala was certainly distinctive, if nothing else. But with the optional 348-cubic-inch V-8 up front, it was also an able-bodied competitor.

Along with the impressive grille, Exner's 613 clay model had also carried truly garish fins, and a less-than-tasteful simulated spare-tire carrier on the deck lid, features that would appear soon enough on regular-production models. But for 1957, the finned 300C was as classy and crisp as anything to roll out of Detroit. Referring to "the most powerful American production car" label given Chrysler's letter cars in 1955, *Motor Life* claimed that "the 300C carries the title even more gracefully than its illustrious forebears." It also carried a wider variety of paint schemes with choices including Cloud White, Jet Black, Parade Green, Copper Brown, and Gauguin Red.

Replacing the Imperial grille borrowed by both the C-300 and 300B, the 300C's massive frontal fascia was exclusive to Chrysler's letter cars and was flanked by a pair of functional ducts that fed cool air to enlarged drum brakes featuring 251 square inches of swept area, up from 201 square inches the previous year. Above the ducts, quad headlights were included

for the first time, although not all 300Cs featured four headlights, thanks to various state laws prohibiting them—all '57 Chrysler fenders were able to mount either single- or dual-headlamp arrangements.

While braking area increased, wheel diameter shrank from 15 inches to 14. But the big news was the 300C's suspension. Along with the car's lowered center of gravity, Chrysler's torsion-bar front suspension assisted handling, although the 300C remained as Detroit's roughest rider in the luxury ranks. Forty percent stiffer than comparable New Yorker units, the 300C's front torsion bars were followed by beefed-up leaf springs in back, themselves 50 percent stronger than standard New Yorker leaves.

Equally newsworthy was the new 392-cubic-inch hemi, a poked-and-stroked version of the 354. Like the 354, the 392 featured a potent solid-lifter cam, a hardened crankshaft, dual valve springs, and twin four-barrel carburetors. Compression for the standard 375-horsepower 392 was 9.25:1; a more radical cam

Although some claim it first appeared the previous year, official Chevrolet paperwork didn't mention an optional four-speed stick for passenger-car applications until late in 1959. Whatever the case, Chevy can lay claim to Detroit's first modern floor-shifted four-speed for regular-production models. Corvettes had featured a four-speed stick beginning in 1957.

and an increase to 10:1 compression helped the optional hemi produced a whopping 390 horsepower, leaving little doubt why the ever-present McCahill described the 300C as "the most hairy-chested, fire-eating land bomb ever conceived in Detroit."

Zero-to-60-mile-per-hour clockings dropped to 7.7 seconds for the 300C, while quarter-mile times as low as 16.9 seconds were recorded. And although NASCAR competition was a thing of the past for the Chrysler 300 following the infamous AMA ban of 1957, a privately campaigned 300C once more took home flying-mile honors at Daytona during the 1957 Speed Weeks trials, hitting 134 miles per hour.

A nearly identical carryover save for smaller taillights (ironically only partially filling the same mounting area used in '57) and a slightly revised grille on some later models, the 300D of 1958 found few buyers, perhaps demonstrating the presence of the typical "what have you done for me lately" attitude among potential

customers, who failed to recognize that the fourth-edition 300 was every bit the brute the 300C was, and more. Cost may have had something to do with the weak response; base price for the 300D hardtop was $5,173, while the convertible started at $5,603. Total 300D production was only 809—588 hardtops (plus 30 exports) and 187 convertibles (and another four exports).

Just as 300 exterior appearances continued basically unchanged, so, too , did the beauty beneath the skin. Brakes remained big—second only to Lincoln in total swept area—and the Torsion-Aire suspension was again as stiff as it got, luxury line or otherwise. Up front where it counted, the 300D's standard 392 hemi received a compression boost to 10:1, resulting in another output increase, if only on paper. Although the 300D's 392 hemi was rated at 380 horsepower, it was no match for the 300C's brutish 375-horsepower 392, thanks basically to revised cam timing intended to make the 300D easier to live with in everyday operation.

Offered after four years of experimentation, a fuel-injected hemi made up the 300D's top perfor-

Chevrolet's 348-cubic-inch "W-head" V-8 featured a distinct wedge-shaped combustion chamber common to almost all engines outside Chrysler Corporation in the '50s. Most uncommon about its design, however, was the way that wedge was formed. While almost all engines feature combustion chambers formed within their cylinder heads, the 348's chambers were created by cutting the cylinder block at an angle, instead of perpendicular. Notice that the face of the cylinder head is essentially flat; the combustion chamber itself exists within the cylinder bore.

Chevrolet offered optional fuel injection for its passenger cars from 1957 to 1959, with latter examples being extremely rare—only a handful are known today. The small badges behind each headlight tell the tale of this almost unheard-of '59 Impala convertible fuelie.

mance option. Rated at 390 horsepower, this 392 V-8 featured—you guessed it—the ill-fated Bendix Electrojector fuel-injection system. Not many buyers felt the 10 additional horses were worth the $400 asking price, and once troubles arose, Chrysler issued a recall and replaced nearly all the Electrojector units with the typical dual-carb intake. Reportedly, only 16 fuel-injected 300Ds were built, and legend has it only one escaped the refit.

As for comparative figures, *Road & Track*'s hotfoots managed 0–60 in 8.4 seconds at the wheel of a 380-horsepower 300D, then tripped the lights at the far end of the quarter mile 7.6 ticks later. In sanctioned competition, Norm Thatcher's 300D set a new Class E speed record on the salt at Bonneville, topping out at 156.387 miles per hour, proving the beautiful 300D was still a brute.

When Chrysler's fifth letter car appeared for 1959, it looked an awful lot like its predecessor, which had looked an awful lot like its predecessor. As was the case with the 300D, the 300E was a slightly revised version of the once-startling '57 300C. A restyled grille and a few trim baubles up front, combined with an updated tail treatment featuring new

A sexy convertible joined the powerful Chrysler 300 line-up in 1957. Appearing here is the droptop 300E of 1959, the year Chrysler traded its vaunted hemi (which had hit 392 cubic inches in 1957) for a typical wedge-head V-8. Displacing 413 cubic inches, the 300E's big wedge was rated at 380 horsepower. *Courtesy Chrysler Historical*

taillights, redesigned fins, and a re-arranged bumper helped set the 300E apart from the 300D, although few innocent bystanders really noticed the differences. As a Chrysler executive told *Car and Driver* in late 1961, "In 1959 we used the same formula because we felt the car was unique and didn't need drastic modification."

Drastic or not, modifications were present, some better-received than others. Inside, leather upholstery was still standard, but by 1959 it had become "Living Leather," a unique woven texture intended to improve comfort in hot conditions. Helping improve both driver and passenger comfort while entering and exiting were the 300E's standard swivel seats, an intriguing bit of gadgetry that came off more as a curiosity than a practical feature.

Of special notice to performance fans was the hemi's demise as the 300D's big 392 was replaced by the lighter 413-cubic-inch Golden Lion wedge-head V-8. Armed with 10.1:1 compression, the 300's trademark dual carburetors, and hydraulic lifters in place of the hemi's mechanical pieces, the new 413 wedge was offered in only one form for the 300E, advertised at 380 horsepower. Gone with the hemi was the optional three-speed stick and the wide range of rear axle ratios. Like the C-300, the 300E came only with an automatic transmission; in this case, the durable three-speed Torqueflite. Backing up the pushbutton-controlled automatic was either a 3.31:1 or 2.93:1 rear end.

Although many missed the hemi, both for its brute force and its impressive image, the 413 was no slouch, and in fact proved capable of rivaling its 392 predecessor, thanks in part to the 100 less pounds it had to carry around—those hemi heads were considerably heavier than their wedge counterparts. *Sports Car Illustrated* reported a 0–60 time of 8.7 seconds and quarter-mile performance of 17.2 seconds at 92 miles per hour for the 380-horsepower 300E.

According to *Speed Age*'s Al Berger, the 300E was "a worthy successor to the models which dominated American stock-car competition in 1955 and 1956." Nonetheless, only 690 were sold—550 hardtops and 140 convertibles. With performance options limited and memories of past competition glories fading fast, the idea of an overly expensive muscle-bound luxury machine no longer seemed viable. Even though *Motor Trend* labeled the 300E

Motor Trend editor Walt Woron (left) shakes hands with Pontiac Motor Division general manager Semon "Bunkie" Knudsen after awarding PMD with *MT's* annual "Car of the Year" award for 1959. Earning that award were the all-new "Wide Track" Pontiacs. *Courtesy Pontiac Motor Division and the Paul Zazarine collection*

1959's "best-looking hardtop," potential buyers stayed away in droves. Even after praising the 300E, *Speed Age*'s Berger found himself wondering if Chrysler had "'gone about as far as they can go' in the development of the large, super-powered automated American car."

Chrysler had—at least as far as the '50s were concerned—but what came afterward in the '60s would quickly have the American car-buying public forgetting all about most of what happened before. For that tale, however, you'll have to tune in same time, same channel, next decade.

INDEX